New Direction
The Study of Reading

New Directions in the Study of Reading

Edited by

Margaret M. Clark

The Falmer Press
(A member of the Taylor & Francis Group)
London and Philadelphia

UK The Falmer Press, Falmer House, Barcombe, Lewes, East Sussex, BN8 5DL

USA The Falmer Press, Taylor & Francis Inc., 242 Cherry Street, Philadelphia, PA 19106-1906

First published in 1985

Library of Congress Cataloging in Publication Data

Main entry under title:

New directions in the study of reading.

Includes index.
1. Reading—Addresses, essays, lectures. 2. Reading readiness—Addresses, essays, lectures. I. Clark, Margaret Macdonald.
LB1050.N359 1985 372.4 85-6756
ISBN 1-85000-069-7
ISBN 1-85000-068-9 (pbk.)

Typeset in 10½/12 Plantin by
Imago Publishing Ltd, Thame, Oxon

Jacket design by Leonard Williams

Printed in Great Britain by Taylor & Francis (Printers) Ltd, Basingstoke

Contents

General Editor's Preface

The study of reading has become both a specialist pursuit and of international concern. A glance at the papers collected under the able editorship of Margaret Clark in this volume amply demonstrates this. But much more than this has been achieved in this reader; the anatomy of thinking about reading has been laid bare in the work of distinguished and eminent scholars.

Each contribution sheds light on an aspect of what reading is, on how one learns to read and may best be taught to read. No longer can reading be thought of in simple terms, as an elementary skill to be acquired; one among a few basic skills on which the whole edifice of one's education can be erected. Far from it. Reading is clearly related to a complex of cognitive and linguistic capabilities. It is at the crossroads of the world as given, a natural entity, and the world as worked on by man. It is into this human world of accumulated knowledge and wisdom, insight, understanding, sensibilities and feelings that reading takes one. It is on understanding the nature of such a voyage that this book embarks; from speech to the beginnings of reading and from there to the amazement of creativity. And a voyage in company with the ordered competence that each contributor brings to bear on one or other aspect of understanding reading. No longer is it other than naive to ask, what is the best approach to the teaching of reading? The issue is, how best does one come to understand what reading is?

It is in addressing this question that this book is successful. It is a book for every student of reading — one might say for every educationist. Reading is all pervasive in what teachers do and in what we all, young and old do, as we seek to learn. This too is a message of this book. In her committed way, in her work with students and in her contacts with scholars worldwide, Margaret Clark endorses this. In this reader she makes this, and much more, very evident and we should be grateful.

Philip Taylor
Birmingham,
July 1985

Editor's Note

About half of the papers in this book had already appeared in print between 1972 and 1984. Some are now either out of print, or are difficult to obtain. Work by the following authors has been reprinted here, (in two instances, Jansen and Blank, in a slightly abridged form):

Section I	John McInnes
	Margaret Donaldson and Jessie Reid
	Marion Blank
Section II	John Downing
Section III	Emelia Ferreiro
	Uta Frith
Section IV	John Pearce
	The paper by John Merritt is a revised paper based on his earlier 'Intermediate Skills'
Section V	Mogens Jansen

The work of most of the above authors was known to the remaining writers who were invited to contribute original papers. Two of these writers were master's level students of the Editor taking a course on reading, Wendy Sutton and Margaret van Lierop. Two others were doctoral students of the Editor, Jennifer Barr and Geoffrey Lewis. The remaining contributor, Max Kemp, Past President of the Australian Reading Association, is also personally known to the Editor as having a range of interests on literacy which would extend the coverage of the book and at the same time relate well to the other contributions. My grateful thanks to all those who have agreed to their work being included in this collection.

Acknowledgements

The Publishers are grateful to the following for permission to reproduce copyright material:

BLANK, M. (1982) 'Language and school failure: Some speculations about the relationship between oral and written language', in FEAGANS, L. and FARRAN, D.L. (Eds) *The Language of Children Reared in Poverty*, chapter 4. Copyright 1982, Academic Press, (in a form shortened and modified by the author for this publication).

DONALDSON, M. and REID, J. (1982) 'Language skills and reading: A developmental perspective' in HENDRY, A. (Ed.) *Teaching Reading: the Key Issues*, Heinemann Educational for UKRA.

DOWNING, J. (1979) *Reading and Reasoning*, chapter 1, W. and R. CHAMBERS Ltd.

FERREIRO, E. (1980) 'The relationship between oral and written language; The children's viewpoint in GOODMAN, Y.M., HAUSSLER, M.M. and STRICKLAND, D.S. (Eds) *Oral and Written Language Development Research: Impact on the Schools*, reprinted with the permission of the National Council of Teachers of English.

FRITH, U. (1982) 'Cognitive processes in spelling, and their relevance to spelling reform', *Spelling Progress Bulletin*. Copyright 1982, reprinted with permission of the publisher.

JANSEN M. (1984) 'Language and concepts: Play or work? Seriousness or fun? Basis or creativity?', *International Research in Reading*, 1, 1., International Reading Association, (in a shortened version).

MCINNES, J.A. (1973) 'Language prerequisites for reading', in CLARK, M.M. and MILNE, A. (Eds) *Reading and Related Skills*, Ward Lock Educational.

PEARCE, J. (1972) 'Literacy is not enough', *Cambridge Journal of Education*, 2, 3.

Introduction: New Directions in The Study of Reading

Margaret M. Clark

In recent years there has been a growing awareness of the insights on learning to read to be gained from close observations of young children's earliest interactions with print. A greater appreciation of the contribution of the home, at the pre-school stage and beyond, and of the out of school environment, to children's literary development is gradually becoming evident.

Textbooks on reading published in the sixties tended to represent the teaching of reading as a skill taught almost exclusively in the first few years in school, thereafter practised, extended and developed into silent reading for comprehension. The emphasis in the instruction of young children in reading tended to be on enabling them to decode and thus understand representations of spoken language. Gradually greater attention is being directed towards the *process of learning to read* and for different purposes, with detailed analyses of the early encounters with print of young children, and consideration of the skills exhibited by the adult reader. Clay (1972) in her book *Reading: The Patterning of Complex Behaviour* is an example of the first of these developments; Smith (1971) in his book *Understanding Reading* reflects the second. The role of linguistic features even in the task of decoding, and of prediction in reading for understanding, have been high-lighted by writers who have stressed the importance of these to understanding progress in learning to read, and the difficulties of those who fail.

The 'hidden complexities' of print have come under scrutiny and the difficulties resulting from its 'disembedded' nature. The importance of appreciating the relationship between spoken and written language, yet of not oversimplifying this into assumptions of printed language as a visual representation of spoken language, is increasingly being discussed; also its implications for literacy learning.

The relationship between reading and writing is also receiving growing attention often by those who had already achieved eminence for their work on reading (such as for example Clay, 1980; and Smith, 1982).

The importance of cognition in understanding development towards literacy has in recent years been stressed. Children are seen by Donaldson (1978) as hypothesis-testers and rule-users, a view supported by Ferreiro (1982) on the basis of her investigations of young children's attempts to understand what is for 'reading', what is 'drawing' and what is 'writing'. In a recently published (1984) book *Awakening to Literacy* (edited by Goelman, Oberg and Smith) a section devoted to 'Literacy and cognition' has as contributors, Donaldson, Ferreiro, Smith, Olsen and Bruner.

Case studies of young children's encounters with print, with their own comments as important evidence, have provided new insights. Examples of these are Bissex (1980) in her study of her young son's developing literacy in *Gnys at Wrk*, Butler (1975) in her study of her multiply handicapped granddaughter Cushla in *Cushla and Her Books*, and recently Payton (1984) in her report of her young child Cecilia's first encounters with books and environmental print. The dangers of assumptions concerning the relationship between certain deficiencies in the homes of children themselves and failure in learning to read, were highlighted by the present writer in her comparison of the findings of her earlier study of children with reading difficulties (Clark, 1970, reprinted in 1979) and the study of young children who were already reading fluently with understanding and enjoyment on entry to school (Clark, 1976). In the first chapter of *Young Fluent Readers* the importance of considering 'reading in a language context' for an understanding both of young children's developing literacy and of those who have severe and irremedial problems is discussed. In the first chapter of the book by Payton referred to above the present writer provides a more extended review of recent literature on the trends referred to above.

There are also important developments in the study of cohesion in different types of extended text. The differences between 'written language' and text contrived and simplified for the teaching of reading, or for backward readers, necessitate that readers acquire a variety of complex skills if they are to read extended text for enjoyment and information. Increasing evidence from text analysis is revealing the extent to which previously overlooked features of print, both functional and featural, must be mastered and in some instances explicitly taught.

The language of instruction in literacy has also been studied with a growing body of evidence that this may place barriers before some children in their first steps towards literacy in the more formal group setting in school. These and related issues are discussed in a review article by Reid (1983) in which she analyzes the changes in emphasis and the insights of relevance to the teaching of reading over the past twenty or more years.

The various developments referred to above are reflected in the choice of papers for this book. The title of the book itself reflects the changing emphasis from the didactic term 'teaching' of reading with its focus on *instruction* (normally) *in school* to the term 'study of reading'. This is not meant to suggest that teaching is no longer important; it is, however, in line with the mounting evidence that children do not at best come to school ready to learn to read. On the contrary children in a literate print-filled environment arrive in school with a variety of skills of importance to learning to read, not least their oral competence whose level has often been underestimated (see Clark, 1985). They are also already forming hypotheses about reading as an information source, about writing as a form of communication and ways in which it differs from drawing. Their ideas on some aspects will be too generalized, in others too limited, based on their encounters with print at this early stage. Skilled teachers must plan their approach, choice of materials, the sequence of presentation and whole range of print experiences in such a way that the children's encounters challenge their cognitive abilities and help them to test and to confirm their sound hypotheses and reject other 'rules' they have formulated about print based on their as yet limited evidence.

Not only children can benefit by learning from an analysis of their own errors or 'miscues' but teachers also in relation to the teaching of reading and writing (Hunter, 1980). We all make mistakes, the good professional learns from these, tries not to make the same mistake twice, to avoid related mistakes — and is open to learn from new evidence. This does not necessitate abandoning all one's previous beliefs and practices, which would merely place one at the whim of the next new idea to arrive. It does, however, mean continued, or at least periodic, reappraisal of one's practice, and empirical testing within the classroom of possible insights from new evidence on reading and related skills.

The following papers have been written and selected to reflect these developments on the process of learning to read, the relationship of these to oral language development and to writing. They provide a range of perspectives, ideas for further empirical investigations in classrooms, extensive reference lists for further reading, and implications for practice throughout a child's education.

References

Bissex, G.L. (1980) *Gnys at Wrk: A Child Learns to Read and Write*, Cambridge, Mass, Harvard University Press.

Butler, D. (1975) *Cushla and Her Books*, Hodder and Stoughton Children's Books.

Clark, M.M. (1970) *Reading Difficulties in Schools*, Penguin Educational (2nd edn 1979, Heinemann Educational).

Clark, M.M. (1976) *Young Fluent Readers*, Heinemann Educational.

Clark, M.M. (Ed.) (1985) *Helping Communication in Early Education*, Educational Review, Occasional Publication No. 11, University of Birmingham.

Clay, M.M. (1972) *Reading: The Patterning of Complex Behaviour*, Auckland, Heinemann Educational.

Clay, M.M. (1980) 'Early writing, and reading: Reciprocal gains' in Clark, M.M. and Glynn, T. (Eds) *Reading and Writing for the Child with Difficulties*, Educational Review, Occasional Publication No. 8, University of Birmingham.

Donaldson, M. (1978) *Children's Minds*, Fontana/Collins.

Ferreiro, E. and Teberosky, A. (1982) *Literacy Before Schooling*, Heinemann Educational, (UK translation 1983).

Goelman, H., Oberg, A. and Smith, F. (Eds) (1984) *Awakening to Literacy*, Heinemann Educational.

Hunter, C.M. (1980) 'Becoming a better teacher of children with learning difficulties', in Clark, M.M. and Glynn, T. (Eds) *Reading and Writing for the Child with Difficulties*, Educational Review, Occasional Publication No. 8, University of Birmingham.

Payton, S. (1984) *Developing Awareness of Print*, Educational Review, Offset Publication No. 2, University of Birmingham.

Reid, J. (1983) 'Into print: Reading and language growth' in Donaldson, M., Grieve, R. and Pratt, C. (Eds). *Early Childhood Development and Education*, Oxford, Blackwell, Chapter 12.

Smith, F. (1971) *Understanding Reading*, Holt, Rinehart and Winston.

Smith, R. (1982) *Writing and the Writer*, Heinemann Educational.

Part 1. Oral and Written Language: Similarities and Differences

Introduction

All three papers in this section have been published elsewhere; the first two are based on presentations to annual conferences of the United Kingdom Reading Association nine years apart. There is a common theme in all three papers, namely the importance of recognizing the similarity in the linguistic basis of spoken and written language and the equal importance of appreciating that the differences go well beyond that of merely a change of medium. Reading is a 'system of communication' and not a skill or even a 'bundle of skills'. McInnes in his paper expresses concern at the widespread use in North America of teaching materials which have been devised merely to develop particular component skills. Since the 'skills orientation' is so deep-rooted he feels it will be difficult to change the approach so that language development is accomplished 'for and through reading'. For McInnes it is important in achieving such a change that teachers are trained in observing and documenting the child's language behaviour.

Donaldson and Reid express a similar concern at any model of teaching reading which assumes that the right way to learn to read is by learning words one at a time in the hope that if this is successfully accomplished words in a sentence, and in written text, will cause little difficulty. Developments in the psychology of language and thinking are explored in their paper in relation to the teaching of reading. The growing evidence of children's competence as 'hypothesis-testers' and 'rule-users' is noted and its implications for the nature of the written language to which children should be exposed in order to enable them to utilize their linguistic abilities in learning the new skill. The initial encounters should be with written language which is 'coherent, explicit and self-contained'. Donaldson and Reid stress the importance of appreciating the problems faced initially by the child in coping with the 'disembedded nature of the language of print', which is indeed one marked difference between much of the oral language of young children and that of print, the former usually being context dependent for its meaning. The important distinction between narrative text and information text which is less predictable and thus requires to be followed in more precise detail is also noted by Donaldson and Reid, an issue which is considered in great detail by Pearce in a later section. Reading is accorded importance by Donaldson and Reid in its own right and in the development of children's thinking. They feel an excitement and expansion of vision can be gained from narrative text, and, would regard the ability to use information text as critical if the child's learning in the content areas is not to suffer.

The third paper in this section, by Blank develops further the theme of the similarities and differences between oral and written language and the 'hidden complexities' in the latter which present some children with difficulties not always fully appreciated. She also refers to the 'disembedded' nature of written language and to its sustained sequential themes. Most reading involves a study of organized connected text and, as Blank illustrates, even apparently simple stories for young children have a high level of 'implicit connectedness'. She notes the absence of 'non-content' words in much printed material for young children learning to read, and older backward readers and in that context discusses the issue of implicit versus explicit cohesion. She suggests that greater use in reading material for young children of connectives such as, 'but', 'however', 'then' and 'until', might in a number of instances have provided this explicit cohesion. A point she makes of relevance in the teaching of reading is that some of the features of the sustained sequential aspects of written language are to be found in stories which could be read orally, and in dramatic play, which together provide ways of introducing written language conventions in the oral language mode.

These three papers set the context. In the following section aspects of readiness for reading will be explored, both the cognitive and linguistic aspects.

*Language Prerequisites for Reading**

John A. McInnes

Language Development and Reading

On the subject of the relationship of reading and language there seem to be areas of agreement among researchers and educators that promise changes and improvements in school curricula. In a synthesis of papers on language development and reading in *Reading Research Quarterly*, Irene Athey (1971) identifies some areas of agreement among the researchers represented in that volume:

> The overriding principle of agreement may be summarized in the statement that reading is not a 'skill' or even a bundle of skills, but a system of communication. This somewhat trite statement, if taken seriously, has far-reaching implications for education, because it means that reading is not viewed as a 'subject' in the curriculum, not even the subject which receives most emphasis in terms of time and resources. It is viewed as one part of the fabric of living and problem-solving which ought to be the focus of the school's efforts in organization, planning and curriculum. In this view the task of learning to read is not a matter of breaking down the reading task into a number of component skills and determining the order in which these skills should be taught. Instead it involves above all the realization that the printed word is another system of communication analogous to speech.

It has been readily observable, in North America at least, that the teaching of reading has been based to an increasing extent on the assumption that reading consists of a bundle of skills. Teaching procedures have been devised to develop particular components skills. Pub-

* Original published in CLARK, M.M. and MILNE, A. (Eds) (1973) *Reading and Related Skills*, London, Ward Lock Educational.

lishers have produced a host of materials aimed at giving pupils practice with particular skills. The testing of children's reading growth has been limited in many situations to measuring performance on certain skills. Attempts to remedy deficiencies in reading have often been based on the diagnosis of errors that supposedly reveal skill weaknesses. The skills orientation is indeed deep rooted. It would seem that if the child's reading growth is to be seen as part of his growth as a person who uses language, then present practices in teaching reading need reevaluating, modifying and in some cases dismantling.

The isolation of reading as a subject has become easy for schools. Periods of instruction have been set aside in which the content is reading skills. Often in these periods children have learned about reading skills much as they would learn about some other body of information. Because of the availability of many commercially produced skill-building materials, children can be put to work on tasks that are quite unrelated to the general fabric of curriculum. The materials can be handled in such a way that no connections are established to the ongoing development of thought and language in the child.

In the *New York Times*, April 1972, Joyce Maynard, an 18-year-old, looked back at school and particularly at the fragmentation of the curriculum. She reflects:

> We had one fine, fancy new gimmick that followed us from fourth grade through eighth. It was a white cardboard box of folders, condensed two-page stories about dinosaurs and earthquakes and seeing-eye dogs, with questions at the end. The folders were called Power Builders and they were levelled according to colour — red, blue, yellow, orange, brown — all the way up to the dreamed-for, cheated-for purple. Power Builders came with their own answer keys, the idea being that you moved at your own rate and — we heard it a hundred times — that when you cheated, you only cheated yourself . . . there were a dozen . . . abbreviations, TTUM, FSU, PQB — all having to do with formulas that had reduced reading to a science. . . . By seventh grade, there was a special Development Reading class. (Mental reading, we called it.) The classroom was filled with audio-visual aids, phonetics charts, reading laboratories. Once a week, the teacher plugged in the speed-reading machine that projected a story on the board, one phrase at a time, faster and faster. Get a piece of dust in your eye — blink — and you were lost.
>
> There were no books in the Developmental Reading room — the lab. Even in English class we escaped books easily. . . . All through high school, in fact, I read little except for magazines. Though I've started reading seriously now, in college, I still find myself drawn in bookstores to the bright covers and shiny, power-

> builder look. My eyes have been trained to skip nonessentials (adjectives, adverbs) and dart straight to the meaty phrases (TVPQM). But — perhaps in defiance of that whirring black rate-builder projector — it takes me three hours to read 100 pages.

Testing programmes in schools have tended to reinforce thinking about reading as a bundle of skills. In discussing measurement in reading Farr and Tuinman (1972) point out that researchers may state that reading is 'that collection of behaviours operationally defined by the test'. They suggest that in research on reading, operational definitions which relate the measure used to observables and/or abstractions outside the measure itself are essential. A circular and limiting effect has occurred where the school has viewed tests as setting out the behaviours that compose reading. The use of results of some reading tests has concealed factors in the child's language that need attention. Often the tests have revealed deficits in the child's reading performance that cannot be overcome without adequate consideration of his language development. Schools have neglected to look further than the results of reading tests in developing programmes for reading improvement.

Wilkinson (1971) has made this statement:

> Learning to read is also, and centrally, a matter of language. Unless he has some language already, the child cannot read language. All the other variables in the situation, important though they may be, must be subordinate to this fact. Certainly 'reading readiness tests', for example, contain linguistic items — vocabulary, word matching, remembering the sequence of words in a story. But such tests tend to concentrate on vocabulary rather than syntax; they do not look at the child's knowledge of language, his awareness of the possibilities of language. . . . It would seem that a systematic study of reading and prereading oracy is one of the most important of our tasks over the next few years.

While schools use reading tests considerably in measuring the pupil's progress in reading, teachers recognize that these tests do not explain sufficiently the child's responses to reading. The teacher needs to reflect continuously on evidence of the child's language development to account for his reading growth. How well can he recall and restate an idea he has read? How well can he summarize a number of ideas from one source or from a number of sources? How well can he compare ideas within an article or between the article and his knowledge of reality? Often the child's failure to respond to reading suggests inadequate language ability prerequisite to the task. Has the child had sufficient experience synthesizing ideas in oral discussion to bring such a strategy to bear on the reading task? Has he had sufficient experience with concrete experiences where comparison was demanded to read critically? Can he bring the mind set and the language of comparison to reading tasks? The school's answer to the child's poor performance has often been to teach skills for which the child had insufficient oral language development.

> Again we become aware of the work children have to do (through language) before they can draw on the mature writer. If their talk and writing in the role of spectator does not reach occasionally beyond the level of gossip, how can they be expected to reach up beyond that level into what the play, or the novel is saying. Yet it is at the level of gossip that we all start, and with many children the classroom offers them their only chance to move towards a fuller sense of what talk and reflection can offer. (Dixon 1967)

Testing programmes have often determined instructional procedures in reading. It is impossible to describe numerically the child's appreciation of what he reads, the intensity of his interest in reading, the success he experiences in using reading as a way of extending his real and imagined worlds, or his growing taste in literature. What can be reduced to statistical description has often been given precedence over these more elusive aspects of growth in reading.

The problem of changing school programmes so that they will accomplish language development for and through reading is not easily solved. Teachers often lack confidence in their intuitions about developing programmes. They have not been told clearly enough that:

> If there is one generalization that can be made from research on developmental linguistics to date, it is that young human beings will have little trouble learning and producing language that is instrumental for goals that they see as important. (Entwisle 1971)

Pre-service and in-service development of teachers needs to emphasize this generalization so that the teachers can recognize and resist forces that drive them in the direction of isolating the reading act from the rest of the child's growth and lead them to use procedures which have little relevance to the child.

Smith (1971) in *Understanding Reading* says:

> The current instructional methods are probably not much inferior to the methods we shall develop as we learn more about learning to read. So many instructional methods have been tried, and so many succeed (in some instances at least), that further permutations in the game of instructional roulette are unlikely to produce any great gain, either by chance or design. What will make a difference is an understanding of the reading process.

Ways of working with teachers to develop this understanding of the reading process need exploration. The work of teacher developers would seem to be to nurture in the teacher a continuing desire to enquire into the process of language acquisition and reading. While the teacher needs to be informed about models of reading and language set out by researchers, she also needs to be able to observe and record development as it occurs in the children with whom she works. She needs to be trained in observing and documenting the child's changing language behaviour. At the same time she needs to examine the situations she develops in school to determine which of these are productive in helping the child grow as a user of language.

Schools and teachers will accept new descriptions of reading as a system of communications, will discard practices that isolate reading as a subject, will develop programmes to provide for the child's growth in reading as part of his language development, if they can be reassured and guided by authorities in the fields of reading research and curriculum change. Efforts to provide better instruction in reading call for increasing and closer contact of researchers and developers who generate new knowledge about reading and language with teachers who have intimate knowledge of children, their needs, and their potential.

References

ATHEY, I. (1971) 'Synthesis of papers on language development and reading', *Reading Research Quarterly* 7, 1, p. 11.

DIXON, J. (1967) *Growth Through English*, London, Oxford University Press.

ENTWISLE, D.R. (1971) 'Implications of language socialization for reading models and for learning to read', *Reading Research Quarterly* 7, 1, p. 151.

FARR, R. and TUINMAN, J.J. (1972) 'The dependent variable: measurement issues in reading research', *Reading Research Quarterly* 7, 3, pp. 413–23.

MAYNARD, J. (1972) *The New York Times Magazine*, 23 April.

SMITH, F. (1971) *Understanding Reading: A Psycholinguistic Analysis of Reading and Learning to Read*, New York, Holt, Rinehart and Winston.

WILKINSON, A. (1971) *The Foundations of Language, Talking and Reading in Young Children*, London, Oxford University Press.

*Language Skills and Reading: A Developmental Perspective**

Margaret Donaldson and Jessie Reid

The last two decades have seen important changes in ideas about the nature of the processes that are involved in reading. These have not been independent of changes in ideas about language and about thinking — indeed about the whole nature and development of the human mind — and they cannot be properly understood without some consideration of this wider setting.

In this paper the early stages of reading are our principal concern, and we shall therefore focus on developments in the psychology of language and thinking that are relevant to them. We shall consider throughout what is implied for teaching and we shall look for pointers to the future.

Views about the reading process — and hence about how to teach reading — have never been free of conflict. But before the 1960s, and indeed for a very long time before then, one widely prevailing notion ran through even those approaches that appeared, on the surface, to be opposed to one another. It was this: that the primary or basic skills in reading consist in seeing how marks on paper (letter shapes, word patterns) differ from one another; in learning to look at them in the correct orientation; in 'recognizing' them when they are seen again; and in uttering — or at least being able to utter — the speech sounds or the words which the marks stand for. Reading, strictly speaking, was commonly held to entail nothing more. The notion of context, while quite often invoked, was mostly vague and unanalyzed; and though 'reading for meaning' was always seen as a desirable goal, initial apprehension of meaning was thought to come necessarily by way of the spoken words, these having 'acquired meaning' previously when oral language was being learned.

So the idea was that the marks were linked to spoken words which in

* Originally published in HENDRY, A. (Ed.) (1982) *Teaching Reading: The Key Issues*, London, Heinemann.

turn were linked to meanings. But what was the nature of the links and how were these forged? Psychology had a ready answer to offer: the links were formed 'by association' (see, for instance, Anderson and Dearborn, 1952).

In the 1950s and earlier, behaviourist psychology was a powerful intellectual force, particularly in the United Kingdom and the United States, and one of its central tenets was that even the most complex kinds of learned behaviour can be reduced to the functioning of simple associative bonds between a stimulus and a response. Thus the theory is atomistic: that is to say, many small units are involved in these processes of association. Accordingly, behaviourist theories of the learning of *oral* language tended to concentrate on how children came to know the meanings of separate words, not on how they made sense of whole utterances. Little attention was paid to syntax — to the question of the ways in which words may be combined to form sentences. And no attention at all was paid to the question of whether children, at an early age, are able to learn the rules that govern these combinations.

It is easy to see how this kind of theory would strengthen the already well established — and, one might say, common-sense — conception of early reading as a matter of associating separate written words with the appropriate speech equivalents. It followed, of course, that the right way to learn words was one at a time; and that if this learning was successfully accomplished, the business of reading a string of words put together to form a sentence should present little or no extra difficulty. This last belief has turned out to be seriously mistaken, and it seems at first sight odd that so many people took so long to recognize the fact. However, the power of theoretical assumptions can be very strong. Before it could become clear that reading entails more than recognizing words, the prevalent theory had to change.

Change was coming from a number of different sources by the 1950s but we want to mention three people — Piaget, Bruner and Chomsky — as having been particularly influential. Though these theorists differ from one another in some very important respects, they have one thing in common which sets them in sharp opposition to the behaviourists — namely the notion that human beings are highly active and constructive in their conceptual dealings with the environment. Stimulus-response theory regards the learner as largely passive. As Skinner (1957) put it, behaviourism leaves 'no originating control inside the skin'. But Piaget, Bruner and Chomsky in their various ways stress the constructive, hypothesis-testing, rule-generating nature of human thought, perception and language.

Piaget had indeed been doing this for decades before, but it was not until the 1950s that the most relevant parts of his work were coming to be well known in the English-speaking countries. Particularly important for what concerns us here is his insistence that we do more than receive a stimulus — we actively *interpret* it, or, in Piagetian terms, we assimilate it to mental structures which we already possess. At the same time Piaget recognizes that, if we are to adapt successfully, we must also modify our behaviour in order to respect the true properties of the things we are dealing with: we must accommodate to what is there (see, for instance, Piaget, 1955).

Bruner's contribution to the changing intellectual climate in the 1950s came originally from his studies of perception. What he and others in the 'New Look' movement argued was that when we perceive we categorize, so that perceiving is one of the higher mental skills (Bruner, 1957). Furthermore, we do this by making inferences, often unconsciously, on the basis of certain actively selected cues (which Bruner said should really be called 'clues'). And different categories may be more or less accessible — more or less ready to be reached by an inferential leap. In other words, what we see will be influenced by our readiness to see it. If we are very ready indeed to see something, we shall need very few cues to recognize it when it comes along. Also, however, if something else comes along in its place what we may then be ready to do is to fall into error.

So Bruner, though he does not use the same terminology, is saying much the same thing as Piaget does when he insists on the importance of both assimilation and accommodation. Bruner's notion of 'readiness' or 'accessibility' is like the emphasis on assimilation. At the same time, he recognizes that a very great reliance on readiness unbalanced by accommodation to what is actually there is a risky business. As Bruner puts it, we must contrive to be flexible enough about our hypotheses to allow them to be 'easily *infirmed* by sensory input' (our italics). And he points out that subjects under stress may develop 'premature hypotheses' which positively interfere with perception, so that the subjects acquire a kind of 'perceptual recklessness' that leads to much erroneous responding.

The direct relevance of this to reading will not be lost on anyone who has tried to teach children. Its influence on reading theory, however, has perhaps been less widely recognized than that of the third thinker of our triumvirate, Noam Chomsky.

Chomsky was concerned too with our 'readiness' to try out certain kinds of hypothesis. But his interests lay in the nature of language rather than in processes of visual perception, and his main claim was that we are innately provided with knowledge of the *kind* of system which a human language is — knowledge highly specific to language, incidentally, and relatively independent of the other skills of the mind (Chomsky, 1965). Chomsky allowed, of course, that we must discover the details of any given language, but he held that our innate equipment ensures that we have appropriate hypotheses all ready to be tested. Thus we make this discovery with what would otherwise be inexplicable speed and ease.

The hypotheses that Chomsky had in mind when he produced these arguments were not, it must be noted, hypotheses about word meanings:

they were hypotheses about grammar. Chomsky was primarily interested in precisely those aspects of language which child psychologists had previously been apt to ignore. And the impact of his ideas was so great that it led in a very short space of time to a flood of quite new kinds of research — research that concentrated on trying to discover what the child might be doing by way of actively formulating and testing grammatical rules — in short, on the child as grammarian. The preferred method for doing this was to collect and analyze a corpus of a child's utterances, and when this preoccupation was at its height in the late 1960s and early 1970s relatively little attention was paid to what the child might mean by what was said. Also the emphasis was on language production and there was not much interest in the study of language comprehension or understanding.

This imbalance was bound to be corrected in time, and the correction did not in fact take long to come. Early in the 1970s there appeared an article by John Macnamara (1972) which was destined to become very influential. Macnamara disputed Chomsky's claim about the highly special capacity for acquiring language, and argued cogently that children are able to learn language precisely because of certain other kinds of mental skill that they possess, and specifically because they are very good at making sense of the kinds of context in which, typically, they hear language being used. Thus from the non-linguistic context they infer the linguistic meaning.

So we find inference and hypothesis-testing yet again. This had become pervasive in the thinking of the time, serving as a common component in theories that differed very widely in other respects.

In the 1970s, then, in a reaction against the 1960s, the concentration on language production waned, the concentration on syntax waned, and more and more work was done on comprehension and on meaning. And if there is one general outcome to this work as one now looks back, it lies in the realization that, long after the very earliest stages of development, the non-linguistic context of spoken language exerts a powerful influence on interpretation. In other words, children — and indeed adults much of the time — do not interpret the words alone. What they are basically interested in is to understand what people mean, rather than what words mean. They interpret the words in their setting — both the physical setting and the personal setting — to such an extent that we may speak of the language as being embedded in its context (Donaldson, 1978).

While the interpretation of embedded language is going on, it is doubtful to what extent children are conscious of the words they are hearing. It has been proposed, indeed, that young children may have very little awareness of the existence of separate words, and that their linguistic awareness in general may be quite limited. One way to put this claim is to say that language is something which they 'see through' to get to the meaning. It is not opaque, and so cannot be looked *at*, cannot be turned into an object of study.

However, the arguments that support this view tend to relate more to the understanding of language than to its production, and may represent too simple a position to do justice to the complexities of language development. If children are concerned *only* with the communication of meaning, how do they learn enough about the structures of language to use them in their own speech? And there is an even more telling question: why do they go on refining their knowledge of these structures long after they know enough for successful communication?

These reflections have led some psychologists — notably Melissa Bowerman (in press, a) and Annette Karmiloff-Smith (1978) — to argue recently that children must have a disposition to discover structure and regularity in language in a manner independent of any immediate communicative purpose, or, as Annette Karmiloff-Smith puts it, that children are disposed to treat language as a problem-space in its own right, something which they 'work on' spontaneously.

Bowerman (in press, b) gives many interesting examples of 'late errors', errors having their onset after age 4 or 5, as evidence that children continue to work away at the more complicated aspects of grammar. Thus one of her daughters, at age 6:10, invited her to 'feel your hand to that' (cf. 'put your hand on that'), while another daughter, at age 5:3, spoke of 'trying to rob the shirt' ('trying to rob me of the shirt').

We now go on to consider how the recent evidence and theorizing about language relate to the question of learning to read.

It is true beyond doubt — it is indeed a tautology — to say that written language is a form of language; and hence it is certainly true that the process of learning to read must be regarded as a process of acquiring linguistic skill. Learning to read is learning to comprehend language expressed through a new medium. However, the acceptance of this truth may lead people to draw two further conclusions — or perhaps rather to make two assumptions. The first is that the ways in which we learn to read are just the same as the ways in which we learn to understand oral language. The second is that the language of books is just the same as oral language, only the medium having changed. We believe that both of these assumptions are false, and that both of them are educationally misleading.

In the first place, as we have already said, everything that is now known about the comprehension of speech suggests that non-linguistic context contributes most importantly to the deriving of meaning. We all make use of this context all the time in normal conversation; and the younger the child the greater the reliance upon the evidence as to meaning which context provides. However, when the words are printed upon a page instead of being spoken by a living person, this kind of evidence is no longer available. It is true that there may be pictures on the page to give some kind of clue, but they are poor substitutes for the hand that points, the voice that rises and falls, the face that frowns or smiles. And, most important of all, what is now inevitably lacking is the familiar sense of ongoing purpose which informs nearly all normal human conversation.

These considerations make it very clear that the tackling of print calls for quite new modes of thought and new kinds of interpretation. Print is essentially disembedded. And when a child first encounters it he has to come to the understanding that he must now rely on the text alone. And this is quite strange and new. It is not surprising that children at first often look at the teacher's face instead of looking at the page, as if they could still find clues to meaning there, just as they have been used to doing in the whole of their lives until then.

Thus children do not — indeed cannot — learn to read in precisely the same ways as they originally learned to understand speech. But on the other hand, once they come to appreciate the general nature of the reading activity, they can, and assuredly do, bring their previously acquired linguistic knowledge to bear on the learning of this new skill. Their 'readiness' to perceive a particular word (to go back to Bruner's terminology) is then a function of their knowledge of grammar and of what they anticipate will 'make sense' — that is, it depends on both syntax and semantics. In other words (Piagetian words this time) they construct meaning by assimilating what they see on the page to the mental structures that they already possess. They make inferences from limited cues. If you like, they guess.

Error analysis reveals this to be true beyond any doubt. The work of Marie Clay (1969) and Rose Marie Weber (1970), showing how high a percentage of early errors fit the preceding syntax, is widely known. But now another question arises: is this guessing 'a good thing'? Is it to be encouraged? Suppose, for instance, that a child looks at the words 'bread and honey' and says 'bread and jam'. Is such a child reading satisfactorily?

It will be obvious that this question relates to the subject that we now know as 'miscue analysis' (Goodman, 1969). But let us rephrase it in the context of our foregoing discussion.

How should a teacher view what is, in Bruner's terms, an example of 'perceptual recklessness', and in Piaget's terms an example of assimilation unbalanced by enough accommodation, yet is a response arising clearly from an attempt on the child's part to make sense of a written message, by using both her knowledge of sentence structure and her knowledge of what sort of thing gets put on bread and tastes good?

It is precisely on this point that some modern views of reading are sharply divided from others. There are those who believe that the kind of substitution in our example is hardly to be regarded as an error at all (see, for instance, Goodman and Burke, 1978). There are others who believe that children must learn to read substantially what is on the page (Ehri and Wilce, 1980). We hold to the second of these views, but we hold to it in full allegiance to the notion that reading involves the construction of meaning from text.

We have already referred to the fact that the kind of non-linguistic context that is always there to support the comprehension of speech is not there to support the comprehension of print. So, in order to understand, the reader has to construct a context in his own mind, and he has to do this from a fusion of what he already knows and what the written language tells him. What he selects from his stock of knowledge in order to construct this context must depend, if it is to be appropriate, on the cueing and the guidance he gets from the text. That is to say, the reader will to some extent interpret in terms of his own experience; but we would argue strongly that what he interprets has got to be, as far as can be achieved, what the author of the text wrote in the first place. Another way to say this is to say that the reader must *respect* the text. And it adds up to an assertion that accuracy, at the level of words, ultimately matters.

The belief that it matters comes from something much more profound than the notion that it is good for children to learn to get things right. It has to do with the nature and purpose of literacy in the history of the development of the human mind (Olson, 1977). One of the main things about written language is that it enables us to be precise; and it does this partly because it preserves its message intact through time, and unchanged in spite of being passed from one recipient to another. Everything transmitted in an oral tradition is changed. We have no idea, for instance, what the original versions of any of our folk-tales might have been. But the works of Aristotle have come down to us as he wrote them.

This property of the written word is one of its main contributions to all disciplined and systematic human learning, learning in which precision plays a crucial part. And the scope that it gives is not only to the thinking reader, but to the thinking writer. Mature reading has been described as 'externally guided thinking' (Neisser, 1967) but mature writing is 'thinking with a pencil in one's hand'. Being able to put our thoughts on paper makes it possible to reflect, to edit, to revise, to restructure, and to take time, without the fear that the thoughts will seep away like water into sand.

One of the branches of study that the written word makes possible is the study of language itself. You can learn to speak a language without the aid of a book, but it is almost impossible to study one systematically without writing it down. At a more humble, yet significant level, children at primary school are encouraged both to do various kinds of writing, creative or fact-based, and to do 'word study' — to look at text and try to see how writers have achieved their effects, to ask why one word rather than any other is just right in its particular place, to become sensitive to nuances and familiar with precise meaning. Here, too, language and thinking are interwoven and influence one another. Much recent work on linguistic awareness — on the child's ability to treat language as an object of reflection and study — suggests that this ability develops greatly between the ages of 5 and 9 or 10 (Scholl and Ryan, 1980). But if this reflective work is to be done on written language it has to depend on the ability to look closely at what is there.

Over recent years, then, we have come to a new understanding of what is entailed in starting to learn to read. We now recognize the significance of the fact that children come to school knowing a good deal about oral language, even though much of the knowledge is not accessible to consciousness in any way that would enable them to speak about it. Secondly, we have come to see children as hypothesis-testers and rule-users by nature. Thirdly, we realize what a strong drive they have to make sense of what they encounter, to understand what people mean when they speak, and what other people's purposes are. And fourthly, we see that the ways in which language becomes meaningful are more subtle and complex than we once supposed.

But we now also know that children may come to school knowing very little of the nature and purposes of written language (Reid, 1966; Downing, 1970). They may need help in forming initial concepts about a writing system. Once they understand that writing carries messages, they will bring their oral language competence to bear on reading; but they will then need help in dealing with the differences between listening to speech and reading print. And these differences are not to be looked on merely as obstacles to progress. They are intrinsic to the nature of written language and to the reasons why learning it is worthwhile.

How, then, in the light of these ideas, should children in the early stages be helped?

It seems very clear that first encounters with print should be with suitable kinds of real written language. With one exception, this means phrases and sentences, and not isolated words. Many 5-year-olds, as we have mentioned, may not be conscious of isolated words, and particularly not of 'function' words which are always enmeshed with the syntax and often slurred over and run together when spoken. The exception referred to above is the case of what we can call 'public print'. It includes such things as notices, street signs, labels, advertisements, and bus destinations. In many of these, single words (like 'litter', 'hospital', 'exit', etc.) are normal usage. Moreover, public print is the least disembedded of any variety of written language, for it is found on or beside objects and in situations where it provides a permanent message with instant, present relevance. It makes sense. It can thus form a kind of conceptual bridge between speech and print-on-the-page.

The views we have been considering argue for initial teaching efforts directed to helping children to realize and expect that the print-on-the-page will also make sense. Early reading should, we believe, be a co-operative affair between teacher and children; and they should certainly not be led to believe that their first task is to memorize some words which will then magically enable them to 'read a book'. To do this is to deprive them of the chance to use the very skills they are best at — hypothesis-forming and rule-using skills that involve syntax and meaning. It is also, as we have shown, to give them a false expectation of what reading is going to be like.

But at the same time, the way print is set down, in lines with spaces between words, is itself powerfully educative. Marie Clay (1969) lays emphasis on the child's early attempts to match spoken language to written, and we believe, with her, that much of children's growing awareness of word-boundaries and word structure happens through their seeing the written form. The kinds of text that support this early learning are those that build on the linguistic skills and expectations which children have. In addition, many varieties of language-experience work, in which sentences are constructed by children and written down by the teacher, not only produce text with appropriate sentence structure but also give a splendid demonstration of the nature of the writing system — of the spacing out of separate words, of the left-to-right convention, of the identity of individual words and phrases which may be used on repeated occasions. These features can also be pointed to as teachers read aloud to a group.

Within this framework of beginning to make sense of bits of printed language, children can take the first steps towards precision quite soon. For instance, the question can be raised as to whether a certain thing, or person, is mentioned on a given page, or what exactly happened at a certain point in a story or episode, and the suggestion made that we look back and check. There are a multitude of ways in which attention can be directed to particular words or phrases in the context of making oneself more certain about what was said. Slowly, by degrees, written words can become in themselves a focus of interest. Earlier, we mentioned Annette Karmiloff-Smith's view that the oral language progress found in children who already have a basic working competence can best be explained by the notion that words become for them 'a problem-space in their own right'. The interest that children in the early school years can develop in the forms and meanings of written words fits well with her views.

Growing awareness of and familiarity with print can thus develop in ways that allow of the integration of existing skills with knowledge of a new kind, though the achieving of the integration will be harder for some children than for others. Biemiller (1970) traced the progress of a group of beginning readers through three phases, by studying their reading errors. Initially, the errors showed reliance mainly on syntactic and semantic cues from the preceding part of the sentence. The children then moved — some more quickly than others — to a phase in which they were more likely to remain silent if puzzled, and in which errors, though still errors, showed increasing attention to graphic cues from the word itself. Finally the children moved to a phase where the best readers tended to use cues of both kinds with a consequent reduction in errors, but where the poorer readers seemed to revert to reliance on context. Biemiller suggested giving these children reading with no context at all. We believe that help must certainly be given to those who find the integration harder, but not by removing context; rather by finding ways of keeping it present while the powers of perceiving what is on the page are strengthened.

Some of this strengthening can be done just by discussion. Children can benefit much more than we have sometimes realized by having specific difficulties talked about in ways that help to enhance their awareness. For instance, a word read wrongly can be compared with its erroneous substitute by writing them one under the other, and the contrast can be discussed with reference both to word patterns and sentence meaning. Material that systematically highlights features of word structure while requiring the children to attend also to phrase or sentence meaning can be helpful. The material should encourage the right expectancies about variations in the ways sounds and symbols correspond. And it should raise children's awareness of the syntactic information carried in word structure — in plural endings, verb tenses, adverbial suffixes and so on. These kinds of learning are in line with modern views of language acquisition in a way that old-style exercises in 'sounding and blending' were not.

While grammatical cues are of central importance, some grammatical variants can be a source of difficulty if they represent a level of language development which a child has not yet reached. For instance, some children come to school with their knowledge of irregular past tenses of verbs still incomplete. One of us recently found a child who could not read 'held up her hand'. When the phrase was read to her and she was then asked what the lady in the story did, the child said 'she holded it up'. When she was asked to re-read the sentence, she said 'holded' again. This is a clear case in which the child has not 'accommodated' to the standard form; it is, for her, a nonsense word to *produce*, yet she understood 'held' when it was said. A similar kind of difficulty surrounds the use of 'an' before a word beginning with a vowel. Many 5-year-olds still say 'a elephant', 'a apple', etc., and will use these forms when reading aloud. A particular case is presented by the word 'another', which children who are still saying 'a other' may be unable to pronounce, although they understand it. Here the balance between helping children onwards and puzzling them is a delicate one.

So have we answered the question about the child who said 'jam' instead of 'honey'? We have at least implied an answer and it is roughly this: the child was obviously able to make a good 'guess' or 'hypothesis' about an unfamiliar word on the basis of syntax and sense, but what she wasn't doing was testing the hypothesis with a readiness to *infirm* it. Or, alternatively, we might speak of too much assimilation and not enough accommodation in her behaviour. If she was very much a beginner, it could well be justifiable to ignore the substitution. But a point in her reading development would soon arrive where it became important for her to be less reckless, and more prepared to accommodate to what was there.

But to encourage this there has to be an explicit understanding between child and teacher that, if you are trying to solve problems, then pauses, mistakes, self-correction and several attempts are all acceptable. Just such an understanding is the basis of much successful remedial teaching.

It is an encouraging thought that children, as Karmiloff-Smith puts it, continue to 'work on' linguistic forms and usages that they have not mastered. For they have to be in good training when they extend their reading experience beyond the early stages. Once children move — as all must do — away from the simple cadences of childlike prose to the language of books, the need for a grip both on connected meaning and on word structure becomes even more compelling. There is a strong suggestion, in some contemporary views, that a grasp of meaning need not depend on an accurate conscious vision of the print (Smith, 1978) and we agree that it need not always do so. Further, it has been suggested that paraphrasing errors can be taken almost as signs of progress (Goodman and Gollasch, 1980). But children cannot paraphrase something they have not interpreted properly in the first place; and the kinds of expansion of syntactic and semantic knowledge that become necessary as their reading widens require them to read with care.

Consider this sentence, which has a deleted subject in the second clause — a common construction in writing.

> 'Tom followed Dick and waved his flag.'

A child who reads this as:

> 'Tom followed Dick *waving* his flag'

will have preserved the sense, though not the actual words. But now consider this one:

> 'Tom *saw* Dick and waved his flag.'

If this is read as 'Tom saw Dick waving his flag' the sense is not preserved, for the flag-waver is now Dick and not Tom. Thus, while the substitution may not greatly matter in the first case, it matters crucially in the second. The only way in which children can avoid making the mistake that alters the sense is to learn that the verb 'to follow' and the verb 'to see' have differing effects on the syntax. But to learn this they must surely read what is there in the first place. Notice, by the way, that there is nothing difficult about the *ideas* with which these sentences deal. The situations are ones that any 7-year-old could readily understand.

The examples used above were derived from a study done by Reid (1972) on children's comprehension of some syntactic features commonly found in extension readers. She found that in the sentence 'Tom walked in front of Dick and carried a flag', 36 per cent of a group of children aged 7–8 said Dick was carrying the flag. The effect of removing the difficulty be inserting 'Tom' a second time was to reduce this percentage to 19.5.

Similar dramatic reductions in difficulty were obtained by simplifying other syntactic features. For instance, in the sentence:

'The girl standing beside the lady had a blue dress',

Fifty-eight per cent of the children said the *lady* had the blue dress. Simplifying the syntax reduced this percentage to 11.4. In another example the word 'both' preceded two adjectives: 'The princess was both clever and beautiful', which 60 per cent of children interpreted as meaning that there were two princesses! Deleting the word 'both' reduced the percentage of error but, interestingly, only to 35 per cent. One sentence contained a negative *meaning* but no negative *term*: 'If only David had known, the dog was quite tame'. This means David *didn't* know; but 42 per cent of the children said he did. By contrast, only 18 per cent of the group tested on the simplified version — with the negative spelt out — chose the wrong answer.

We believe that a great deal of failure in comprehension and thus much of the disillusionment with reading that occurs in the later primary years has its roots in children's experience of meeting syntax that they cannot process. The language they find in books is saturated with phrase and sentence structures that are not the norm in speech. In fiction, even if we exclude the more ambitious examples of children's literature, there are many stylistic features without which a narrative would be obscure and incoherent, or flat and tedious. In information text there are comparable, though different, ways of using syntax to present facts, describe processes, explain sequences of events, and so on. And because these features have to do with the nature of written language and its need to be coherent, explicit and self-contained, they are not learned through conversation: most are met only between the pages of a book. Moreover, information text is for obvious reasons much less predictable than narrative, and must often be followed in detail.

Children who do not accommodate to these features do not progress in reading. They miss many experiences of excitement and expansion of vision. Their learning in the content areas is seriously crippled. And we would argue further that their very modes of thinking are stunted and confined.

So the move into the language of books becomes a matter for the utmost thought and care. Texts must be looked at for readability with an eye to syntax (which, incidentally, readability indices do not measure very well (Schlesinger, 1969)). And a great deal of support should continue to be given by the teacher through reading aloud. As at earlier stages, this allows new and more complex forms to become familiar to children's ears while the living voice helps to bring out the meaning, with amplification and explanation if needed. The right level of difficulty for text read aloud — which can be some way in advance of the children's reading level — must be achieved by careful selection and not by wholesale simplifying, which would merely destroy the value of the exercise.

Perhaps the most crucial aspect of the move, however, has to do with the kinds of specific help that children can be given in adding new syntactic patterns and new words to their reading repertoire. This is an area of learning that has been until now much neglected; but we have come to believe it is one where direct teaching has an important part to play. The teaching could involve explicit discussion of areas of confusion, or attention to shifts and contrasts in meaning and usage, both in individual words and in larger units. And it is here that the need for precision — for reading what is on the page — becomes very clear. In order to be able to *talk about* a puzzling phrase or sentence, children must be encouraged to come to grips with the actual wording, identify an unknown term or a piece of syntax that refuses to 'gel'. It may mean a temporary move away from seeing 'through the print to the meaning', but the move is a necessary one, and is not, as we have seen, out of line with children's natural tendencies at the ages we have in mind.

Looked at in this way, progress in reading in the middle primary years acquires an enhanced status. It is already recognized as the basis of learning in the content areas and as a source of much enjoyment and enrichment. But we must see it as more than this. We must see it also as the main road, for the child's mind, out of the situation-bound, embedded thinking and language of the pre-literate years into a new kind of mental power and freedom.

References

ANDERSON, I.H., and DEARBORN, W.F. (1952) *The Psychology of Teaching Reading*, New York, Ronald Press.

BIEMILLER, A. (1970) 'The development of the use of graphic and contextual information as children learn to read'. *Reading Research Quarterly*, 6, pp. 76–96.

BOWERMAN, M. (in press, a) 'Starting to talk worse; Clues to language acquisition from children's late speech errors', in STRAUSS, S. (Ed.) *U-Shaped Behavioural Growth*, New York, Academic Press.

BOWERMAN, M. (in press, b) 'Reorganizational processes in language development', in GLEITMAN, L. and WANNER, E. (Eds) *The State of the Art in Language Acquisition*, New York, Academic Press.

BRUNER, J.S. (1957) 'On perceptual readiness'. *Psychological Review*, 64, pp. 123–52.

CHOMSKY, N. (1965) *Aspects of the Theory of Syntax*, Cambridge, Mass, MIT.

CLAY, M.M. (1969) 'Reading errors and self-correction behaviour', *British Journal of Educational Psychology*, 39, pp. 47–56.

DONALDSON, M. (1978) *Children's Minds*, London, Fontana.

DOWNING, J. (1970) 'Children's concepts of language in learning to read', *Educational Research*, 12, pp. 106–12.

EHRI, L.C., and WILCE, L.S. (1980) 'Do beginners learn to read function words better in sentences or in lists?', *Reading Research Quarterly*, 16, pp. 452–76.

GOODMAN, K.S. (1969) 'Analysis of oral reading miscues: Applied psycholinguistics', *Reading Research Quarterly*, 5, pp. 9–30.

GOODMAN, K.S., and BURKE, C. (1973) 'Theoretically based studies of patterns of miscues in oral reading performance', USA, Final Report, Department of Health, Education and Welfare, Project No. 9-0375.

GOODMAN, K.S., and GOLLASCH, F.V. (1980) 'Word omissions: Deliberate and non-deliberate'. *Reading Research Quarterly*, 16, pp. 6–31.

KARMILOFF-SMITH, A. (1978) 'The interplay between syntax, semantics and phonology in language processes', in CAMPBELL, R.N. and SMITH, P.T. (Eds). *Recent Advances in the Psychology of Language*, New York, Plenum Press.

MACNAMARA, J. (1972) 'Cognitive basis of language learning in infants', *Psychological Review*, 79, pp. 1–13.

NEISSER, U. (1967) *Cognitive Psychology*, New York, Appleton-Century-Crofts.

OLSON, D.R. (1977) 'From utterance to text: The bias of language in speech and writing', *Harvard Educational Review*, 47, pp. 257–81.

PIAGET, J. (1955) *The Child's Construction of Reality*. London, Routledge and Kegan Paul.

REID, J.F. (1966) 'Learning to think about reading', *Educational Research*, 9, pp. 56–62.

REID, J.F. (1972) 'Children's comprehension of syntactic structures found in some extension readers', in REID, J.F. (Ed.) *Reading Problems and Practices*, London, Ward Lock.

SCHLESINGER, I. (1969) *Sentence Structure and the Reading Process*, The Hague, Mouton.

SCHOLL, D., and RYAN, E.B. (1980) 'Development of metalinguistic performance in the early school years', *Language and Speech*, 23, pp. 199–211.

SKINNER, B.F. (1957) *Verbal Behaviour*, New York, Appleton-Century-Crofts.

SMITH, F. (1978) *Reading*, Cambridge, Cambridge University Press.

WEBER, R.H. (1970) 'A linguistic analysis of first-grade reading errors', *Reading Research Quarterly*, 5, 3, pp. 427–51.

*Language and School Failure: Some Speculations about the Relationship between Oral and Written Language**

Marion Blank

It has long been known that there is a strong correlation between oral language skills and achievement in the written language domain (see Benton and Pearl, 1978). The relationship, however, is not a simple one largely because of the fact that the two language systems are far from identical.

For example, the sentences you have just read would almost only be experienced in print, and not in speech. Furthermore, if they did happen to be spoken, they would probably never appear as the 'opener' of a conversation — even though they can easily serve this role in the written language realm. This state of affairs presents us with an intriguing problem — namely, how are we to define the nature of the relationship that exists between these overlapping, yet distinctively different systems? It is to this question that the current chapter is addressed. Specifically, the material that will be presented here will be guided by a three-part question:

What are the essential characteristics of written language?

To what degree are these characteristics found in oral language?

To what extent do these characteristics pose problems for children who are experiencing difficulties in mastering reading?

In dealing with the first part of the question — the essential characteristics of reading — I would like to suggest the following five qualities: (a) the disembedded quality of reading; (b) the sustained, sequential aspect of written discourse; (c) the implicit connectedness of ideas; (d) the conventions of written language; (e) the receptiveness of reading. Each of these will be discussed in turn.

* Revised for this publication. Originally published in FEAGANS, L. and FARRAN, D.L. (Eds) (1982) *The Language of Children Reared in Poverty*, New York, Academic Press.

The Disembedded Quality of Reading

The term *disembedded quality* is one that I have borrowed from Margaret Donaldson. In an interesting book entitled *Children's Minds* (1978), Donaldson attempts to define the characteristics of classroom discourse — that is, oral language discourse — that may cause difficulty for many children. The quality that she finds most significant is the abstract, 'decontextualized' character of much of the language exchange. She puts it as follows:

> It is when we are dealing with people and things in the context of fairly immediate goals and intentions and familiar patterns of events that we feel most at home . . . However, when we move beyond the bounds of human sense, there is a dramatic difference. Thinking which does move beyond these bounds so that it no longer operates within the supportive context of meaningful events is often called 'formal' or 'abstract.' . . . To reduce the risk of confusion . . . I shall speak rather of 'disembedded thinking' (with formal being one way of disembedding). The better you are at tackling problems without having to be sustained by human sense, the more likely you are to succeed in our educational system [p. 75 and 77].

Donaldson goes on to claim that a child who can handle the formulation, *If p, then q*, will be more successful than a child who can only deal with the formulation when it is in such terms as *If there are houses, then there are doors.*

Although Donaldson considers oral language exchange, many of her comments are valid for the world of written language as well. Reading by its very nature has a disembedded quality. It generally does not go to the contentless extreme of an *If p, then q* formulation. Nevertheless, even when there are supporting pictures, the ideas in a book do not have the power of an actual event. For example, imagine a child who is at home and hungry. In this situation, he could easily and without much reflection say, *I want a sandwich*, or some comparable request. When a similar event is depicted in a book, the child himself no longer has the internal cues (i.e., the feeling of hunger) or external cues (i.e., the kitchen nearby, a supportive figure who complies with requests, etc.) that meaningfully tie the language to the context. In other words, the language is disembedded from the physical context in which it would naturally occur. This single, simple example is trivial. It is offered here only to illustrate the point that disembedding occurs even in the simplest cases of text. Once text becomes more complex, the disembedding becomes increasingly powerful and significant.

In considering the second part of the question posed — namely, to what degree is this characteristic found in oral language — we find an interesting phenomenon. If one analyzes the verbal interactions involving children, it seems clear that much of the language used by children is embedded and context-bound. For example, a child whose finger is bothering her might say to her mother, *I have got a sore finger*, or a child who wants to put on a particular dress might say *I can wear this*; a child who does not want to get on the school bus says, *I am not going to school.* Disembedding clearly and not surprisingly does not represent a dominant mode of verbal exchange for children (and possibly for few adults as well).

In children who are becoming adept at higher level language skills, however, instances of disembedded language begin clearly to emerge. For example, I recently saw a 4-year-old who was asking his mother about 'how babies are made.' Most surprisingly, from the mother's point of view, his concern was not what she and most adults would have anticipated. As she tried to explain about reproduction, he interrupted and made himself clear by stating, *Not that, I mean: Do they come out just with bones and then someone puts the skin around them?*

The richness of this anecdote allows it to be interpreted in multiple ways. From a Piagetian point of view, it can be used as further evidence for the conceptual limitations of the preschooler. But from the Donaldson point of view, the exchange has major elements of disembedding. There is no immediate physical need or problem confronting the child (i.e., he is not faced with the task of constructing a baby), and there are no contextual cues currently available to support the question (i.e., this particular question was triggered by the child having seen a picture of a human skeleton in an encyclopedia some days before). While this particular question is not nearly as disembedded as an *if p, then q* formulation, it nevertheless appears to have major elements of the decontextualized thought to which Donaldson refers.

If we now turn to the third part of the question guiding the approach being offered here, we confront the problem: To what extent does this quality pose problems for children who experience reading difficulties? Because of the paucity of research in this area, no firm answer can be offered. However, in studies that my colleagues and I have conducted (Blank, Rose and Berlin, 1978) we have obtained evidence that disembedded language, represented by questions requiring such processes as prediction (for example, *What will happen ...?*) and justification (for example, *How did you know...?*), is mastered by children 5 years of age who are likely to succeed in reading but poorly mastered by children who are at risk for failure to read.

The Sustained, Sequential Aspect of Written Language

A second feature of written language is its use of long verbal chains. The term *chain* is *not* meant to represent a behaviorist view of language, but rather the fact that reading involves sentences — with one sentence following another for extended sequences. The sustained, sequential aspect that is so typical of written language is not characteristic of much oral language. As in the examples of children's comments earlier (for example, *I've got a sore finger*, and *I'm not going to school*), much conversation occurs as one or two relatively isolated utterances. Even when the conversation continues, there is no clear demand for maintaining a continuous theme. Hence, after the comment about a sore finger, a bandage might be applied, and that particular topic might end. Essentially, much of oral language might be seen as representing perceptual-verbal connections in that each utterance is tied to a clear physical context. By contrast, much of written language might be seen as verbal-verbal connections because the language at one point is meaningful only insofar as it is tied to language at a preceding point. This distinction is not meant to represent an all-or-none phenomenon; rather it is intended to highlight a feature that generally distinguishes the two language systems.

As in the case of *disembedded language*, conversation at times shows the sustained, sequential aspect of written language. Susan Isaacs (1930), in her reports on pre-school children, has documented the sophisticated skills that can be found in this realm by 4 and 5 years of age. Unfortunately, relatively little attention has been paid to this phenomenon. Considerable research effort in oral language has been devoted to the analysis of language at the level of the word and the sentence, but relatively little at the level of connected discourse. In order to provide some insight into the phenomenon being discussed, the material that follows offers a segment of dialogue between a teacher and a 6-year-old learning disabled boy. A physical object (a book) is present, but the exchange is characteristic of verbal-verbal dialogue in that the language is not tied to a motivating physical context that can elicit the child's active involvement. The book essentially serves as a point of departure for a series of questions, with one question building upon the previous one — hence, a verbal-verbal exchange.

Adult	*Child*
1 *Jim, look at this, we're going to be talking about this book today* (pointing to a wordless book; for example, a storybook based on pictures alone).	2 (picks up pen from table, then glances over at book)
3 *You know, this is a special book. Look through the pages and tell me how it's dif-*	4 (rolls pen around in hand)

ferent from other books (points to other books on table).

5 (takes pen from child) *Let me put this away. You can play with it later.*

6 (picks up a plastic bowl and moves it around the table)

7 *Look through the pages and tell me how you think it's different.*

8 (quickly leafs through pages) *He's fallin' in* (points to picture, then quickly picks up a pen).

As long as the dialogue remained confined to this level, the child remained disinterested. uncomfortable, and taciturn. Once the teacher redirected the exchange so that it involved a perceptual–verbal dialogue (i.e., dramatizing the actions depicted in the book), the child's behavior changed dramatically. The following segment is illustrative of the process.

Adult	*Child*
1 *Let's try and make something that looks just like this picture* (referring to a boy fishing). *Let's first get a bucket* (points to bucket on table) . . .	
	2 (reaches over, moves bucket closer to adult) (This action, in contrast to ones in the prior segment is not an attempt to 'leave' the exchange; rather it reflects a desire to cooperate with the adult's suggestion)
3 . . . *and fill it with some water. Do you see any place in this room where we could get water?*	
	4 (looks around room, then points toward sink) *Yeah, over there.*
5 *Could you go over and fill up the bucket?*	
	6 (goes over to sink

	and fills up bucket, then returns to table)
7 *Now, I'd like you to pour some of that water in this tub* (points)	
	8 (starts to pour water in tub) *All of it?* (this is the first instance in the entire lesson of the child initiating an idea. It further suggests his comfort and freedom in this setting).
9 *That's a very good question. Let's see. How about putting up to this line* (draws a line in the tub).	
	10 *All right* (pours water up to mark) *There's just a teeny bit in there* (referring to remainder left in bucket). (Again the child is initiating his own ideas in the exchange)
11 *Right, there's just a teeny bit left over. Where is most of the water now?*	12 *In there* (points to tub).

These two small segments of dialogue raise interesting questions. The differences in the child's responsivity in the two exchanges might be attributed to motivation so that his seeming limitations in the first segment are seen only as performance variables (for example, fear, disinterest, etc.) and not as a reflection of any limitations in his verbal competence. In this view, the second segment made him more comfortable, thereby allowing his language behavior to emerge and show its strength.

This argument represents an important and complex issue that cannot be dealt with easily. My own opinion is that the motivation is a consequence and not a cause of the language behavior. Specifically, I believe that verbal-verbal, disembedded exchanges are difficult for young children and continue to be difficult for the children with problems in the academic setting. They do not understand the organization and rules by which such exchanges are carried on, and this causes them to feel confused and defensive. By contrast, the realm of perceptual-verbal, embedded exchanges is clear and more easily mastered. In such a dialogue, one does not have to retain what occurred even one or two exchanges earlier. Instead, the physical context serves as a powerful aid so that each utterance seems clear and meaningful in its own right (talking about the water, the bucket, etc.), and no attention need be paid to the continuity among exchanges. To the degree that continuity exists, it is generally a by-product of the physical context remaining unchanged and not the result of the speaker's effort to maintain a consistent theme. If this hypothesis is correct, it suggests that the strength or extent of a verbal skill cannot be evaluated as an independent entity (for example, one cannot ask simply, Can person A produce formulation X?). Instead, the context in which the language is used is a critical variable in assessing the verbal mastery that any person has.

These comments have been designed to suggest that a critical variable in language use is the perceptual-verbal versus the verbal-verbal nature of an exchange. Books by definition represent unusually long and complex verbal-verbal sequences. Hence, mastery of sustained verbal exchanges in the oral language sphere might be a vital precursor to written language mastery.

The Implicitness of Connected Discourse

The past decade has seen a major *paradigmatic* shift in the study of reading. In contrast to the long emphasis on skills of decoding, increasing attention is being paid to the fact that most reading involves organized, connected text. Much of the research effort is now focused on studying how readers comprehend the variety of passages with which they must deal (Walker and Meyer, 1980). Central to this view is the idea that reading involves chains that are linked so as to create a coherent set of ideas. We are only now beginning to appreciate the complexity of processing necessary for recognizing that coherence since the unity is often implicit rather than explicit. Even seemingly simple stories for preschoolers demand high levels of implicit connectedness. For example, consider the following page from a nursery story entitled *Squirrel Goes Skating* (Uttley, 1980). In the story Hare, who lives with Grey Rabbit, is speaking about his chilblain (a type of frostbite):

> 'Ow, ow,!' exlaimed Hare, rubbing his toe. 'Do think of something Grey Rabbit, you don't know how it hurts.'
> 'Moldy Warp once told me to use some snow,' said Grey Rabbit. 'I'll get some.'
> She ran outside and scraped the frost from the grass. Then she rubbed Hare's foot till the chilblain disappeared.

The point to note about this deceptively simple passage is the marked change that occurs in every possible parameter from one sentence to the next. The changes encompass length, vocabulary, syntax, and concepts. For example, in terms of the single dimension of speaker intent (a major pragmatic variable), the first utterance is a complaint, followed by a direct request, which is then followed by an implied request. The second speaker responds by reporting some information that has been obtained from another party (*Moldy Warp once told me . . .*). From a purely logical point of view, it seems unnecessary at best, and foolish at worst, for a listener to respond to a request for help by reporting a bit of information representing a third person's idea. Nevertheless, the reply is not seen as illogical but as sensible and possibly interesting.

For people who are fluent in language, the rapid shifts across sentences go almost unnoticed, and the text seems quite coherent. The reason for the coherence, however, is not based on anything that is said in print but rather on what is not said — what is invisible. Unstated, implicit ideas are available to the sophisticated language user that serve to unify the great variation of form and content in the information actually stated. The 'sense' of written text paradoxically comes as much, if not more, from the unstated than from the stated.

As with the issues discussed previously, there appear to be oral analogues to this process of implicit cohesion. Again, the oral analogues are not high frequency occurrences, largely because so much of everyday dialogue can take place without concern for cohesion. Nevertheless, cohesion can be found, and major elements of the process seem to be mastered by many preschoolers. For example, in a lunchtime conversation between a mother and her 5-year-old child, the mother said, *Now eat your carrots.* Then she paused and, changing tone, said, *Oh, I forgot to plant the tomatoes.* The conversation continued for a while until suddenly the child altered the flow by saying, *I know why you said tomatoes. When you said carrots, it made you think of tomatoes, and that's why you did it.* In effect, the child was saying that she expects a conversation to be connected, that the grouping of tomatoes and carrots in that context was peculiar but that there must be some logic available by which the combination could be explained — and indeed, she found the logic.

Although coherence between utterances is expected and understood by skilled language users, children who are poor in language present quite a different situation. Those who have not attained mastery of verbal-verbal exchanges do not possess the skills by which to connect the seemingly endless and unstructured variety in the material they confront. In the absence of unstated organizing themes, they have little expectancy as to how the text will proceed. For example, if one could ask the nonverbally sophisticated child, 'Which sentence is a more logical one in the exchange between Hare and Grey Rabbit, *She ran outside and scraped the frost from the grass.* or *She ran outside and made some snowballs for throwing?'* it is likely that the child would not see one as preferable to the other. Indeed, the snowball one might be seen as better since it both connects more directly to the word *snow* in the previous sentence and it reflects a more desirable activity.

In my view, the children's difficulties in this area are dependent in large measure on the amount of unstated information that must be gleaned to make the text comprehensible. No text can be totally explicit. If the gaps are fairly small, however, the children can cope more effectively. For example, a narrow gap might be exemplified by the following: After Hare says, *You don't know how it hurts*, Grey Rabbit might have said, *Oh, it does hurt and I will help you so that it stops hurting.* The redundancy of the information and the closer semantic links (*hurt-help*) allow the child to avoid dealing with high levels of implicit information.

The issue of implicit versus explicit cohesion has been generally neglected in early reading. Effort has concentrated so heavily on presenting simple words that can be easily decoded that the connectedness of the text is often even more implicit than it is in books for more sophisticated readers. Much connectedness depends on the use of noncontent words (for example, *but, however, then* and *until*), which relate one idea to another (for example, in the sentence, *Then she rubbed Hare's foot*, the word *then* implies that the activity followed upon Rabbit's scraping of the frost). Because most noncontent words are both deemed meaningless and marked by difficult grapheme-to-phoneme correspondences, they are often specifically avoided in early texts. As a result, the child is faced with establishing cohesion in the absence of many of the most useful and common cues that permit cohesion.

The following first-grade passage (Makar, 1977) illustrates the phenomenon under discussion. Accompanying the text are pictures of a pup (Tag), a cat (Kit), and a girl (Peg).

Tag is a pup.
Kit is a cat.
Kit ran to get Tag.
Peg has a wig.
The wig is wet.
Peg set the wig on a big log.

Although some of the same words reappear (for example, *Tag, Peg, wig,* etc.), they generally do not serve to enhance cohesion. The ideas of each sentence are so independent that the reading of one sentence does not sufficiently prepare the reader for the content of the next (for example, if one were asked to predict the second sentence after reading the first, it seems highly unlikely that the theme, *Kit is a cat*, would be offered). As a result, early texts leave children — particularly children in difficulty — to confront an almost unmanageable linguistic situation. The explicit cues for cohesion are misleading (they repeat content, but the words lack an intrinsic relationship to a theme), and the implicit cues for cohesion are practically nonexistent (the subtle connectives are deleted so that there is no clear organization for relating one sentence to the next). Many of us have long been discouraged by the texts offered to beginning readers. The point emphasized here is that cohesion may be a key factor in explaining our dissatisfaction and, ultimately, in offering better alternatives.

Conventions in Writing

As noted at the outset, oral and written language differ (Hunt, 1977; Moffett, 1968). Although the differences between the two modes of language are readily acknowledged, insufficient recognition has been given to the fact that the conventions employed in the written mode often violate the rules that the child has learned in the oral mode. For example, books for young children typically contain pictures to accompany the text. The pictures are included so as to make the material more appealing to children and thereby ease the transition from oral to written language. To understand the situation facing the child, imagine a picture — for example, a bird singing on a rooftop. Imagine further that the scene being depicted is not in a book, but represents (as it is supposed to do) a real event. Then make up some sentences about the scene. Under these conditions, adults commonly respond with statements such as the following: *There is a bird on a house, That bird is standing and singing,* and *A bird is wearing a hat and singing.* In fact what the book says is: *Mr. Bird* was *happy. He* was *so happy he* had *to sing* [Eastman, 1968].

The words *was* and *had* have been emphasized not because they are unique to this book but rather because they are so typical of children's stories. Although a visual representation is present that in the nonbook world would be described in the present tense, in the book world the past tense is used. This use of the past tense is counter to almost any use of the past tense that the child has learned. Indeed, in reading this page aloud, a learning disabled child read it as, *Mr. Bird is happy, he has so happy.*

These violations of oral language are common in early reading. For example, in the nonbook world when people speak, they simply offer the utterance they have in mind. When their statements are translated into the written mode, they are accompanied by such words as *he said, they shouted,* and *she whispered.* In other words, quotations must be explicitly introduced and identified with devices that generally involve complex pronominal change (for example, *He said: I am going*). The reasons for this are clear and reasonable, but they nevertheless represent distinctly different uses of language from those that occur with spoken language. Furthermore, these altered uses of language occur in the earliest books that children must read.

As before, the question arises as to whether these written language conventions ever appear in the oral language mode. Examination of young children's experiences suggests that there are two major domains in which these conventions are found. One is clearly in story-reading — that is, when adults read stories to young children, the children are clearly exposed to these sorts of language uses. There is a second major domain in which they appear. This is the realm of dramatic play. In dramatic play, children employ a number of devices through which they distance themselves from the language in ways reminiscent of the conventions used in books. For example, as they plan and structure their roles, they commonly switch among verb tenses, they assign quotations explicitly to the various participants, and they do not describe the real world but rather a pretend world (for example, *You said, stand in line. But I'm the teacher, and I'm supposed to say that*).

As might be expected, children who have difficulties in learning to read seem to encounter limitations in both these domains of oral language. For instance, parents of children who function poorly in school commonly report that the children do not enjoy being read to. This is not unexpected in that they are not attracted by long verbal sequences. At the same time, this means that they do learn to deal with the conventions of the written mode. Similarly, these children are also reported to show delay and/or difficulties in dramatic play. Again, they are excluded from a major channel through which their language skills might be enhanced.

The Receptiveness of Reading

One of the major features of language, whether oral or written, is that it represents an act of communication; communication, in turn, involves the participation of at least two persons. One is the speaker who is sending the message and the other is the listener who is receiving the message. Differences, of course, exist. In the written language mode, only one person is present, and during the act of reading, that person assumes essentially only the role of the listener who follows the logic, reasoning, thoughts, and ideas of an invisible speaker.[1]

The importance of the listener role in reading demands the reconsideration of some commonly held views concerning the relation

Note

1 The act of writing also involves the presence of only one person, with that person serving in the role of the 'speaker.' If the writing is to be meaningful and coherent, however, the speaker's role is greatly complicated because he or she must anticipate all the needs, interests, and capabilities of the non-present listener. Hence, writing, like reading, demands that the communication be formulated in the absence of the feedback that is such a major feature of oral communication.

between oral and written language development. Studies of oral language development have tended to value the speaker role more than the listener role; the more complex the language produced by a child, the more advanced is his or her functioning judged to be. The influence of this orientation can be seen in many areas. For example, expressive language is deemed to be more difficult than receptive language, and production is seen as more advanced than comprehension. Some have challenged this view (Clark, 1980; Goodman and Goodman, 1977), but it still continues to exert a powerful influence. Thus, many preschool programs encourage children to speak a great deal since extensive speaking is seen not only as indicative of expressive language mastery but as the foundation for effective reading.

Effective communication in both the oral and written mode, however, cannot occur unless one is willing and able to comprehend the verbalizations produced by another person. This emphasis on receptive language may seem strange since receptive language is thought to be relatively simple. Hence, even if one acknowledges its significance, it might be assumed that almost all children are well equipped for the receptive-listener mode that must be adopted for reading. Research that I and my colleagues have conducted (Blank, Rose and Berlin, 1978), however, has suggested that the discrepancy between expressive and receptive language diminishes, if not disappears, when one controls for problem difficulty. Thus in many tests, receptive language demands are relatively simple (for example, *touch your nose, pick up the pencil*), whereas expressive language demands are more complex (for example, *repeat the story you just heard; tell me how you get to school*). When receptive language demands are formulated so as to be of equivalent difficulty to expressive language demands (for example, *before you touch the chair, I want you to tap the fourth block*), the receptive language skills are not found to be easier than expressive language ones. Indeed, in certain language disorders, receptive language is poorer than expressive language functioning (Blank, Gessner and Esposito, 1979).

This improbable finding becomes less puzzling when one considers the pragmatics underlying expressive and receptive language. Expressive language can occur as an utterance that is unrelated to any other utterance in a conversation. For example, in the opening of a conversation, one may come into a room and ask, *Has anyone seen my coat?* In utterances of this type, one can concentrate on formulating the particular issue that one has in mind and pay relatively little attention to the thoughts or interests of the person who hears the verbalization. Expressive language, however, can also occur as the response to another person's utterance (for example, replying to the question above with a comment such as *Yeh, I think you left it in the car*). Thus, expressive language can take on two forms: One is as an elicited response that is part of a communicative exchange; the other is as an utterance that is far more independent of communicative demands.

By contrast, receptive language always represents an elicited response (for example, pointing to a picture in reply to someone saying, *Show me the dog*). Thus, even though the responder may not use any overt language, he or she is responding to a communicative event. In this sense, elicited expressive language and elicited receptive language are similar communicative acts despite their difference in form. By contrast, non-elicited expressive language (for example, non-elicited in the sense that it is not a reply to another person's utterance) may represent a different, and in many ways, easier behavior. It is easier in the sense that when using this type of language the child 'is spared the task of putting himself in the other person's position ... The spare attention ... then may be used for formulating' relatively more complex utterances [Clark, 1980, p. 16]. In other words, the child's comprehension (for example, where he or she has to both understand language and interpret another person's position) may be less sophisticated than production (for example, those instances of production where he or she can concentrate on the language alone).

The pattern of the discussion until now has been to ask if children who have difficulty in mastering the reading process also show difficulty in the area of oral language under consideration. Unfortunately, because of the paucity of studies of language, little information can be offered at this time about children's ability to deal with the demands of 'receptive' language. We have begun to study this issue in our research (Blank and Franklin, 1980), and hopefully, in the not too distant future, a richer data base will be available. In the interim, it seems important to recognize that the trend in both psychology and education is not only to minimize the significance of 'elicited' language skills but actually to view them as counterproductive to a child's sense of self. For example, when a child displays difficulty or disinterest in attending to the language of others, this behavior is often rationalized with the statement, *He just wasn't interested, that's all.* or *Why should he have to listen? He has the right to decide whether or not he wants to get involved.* As in the issues considered earlier, this view has validity: Children cannot be viewed simply as individuals who are to be dominated by others. But to the degree that the behavior represents a pervasive attitude toward situations involving elicited language, then the child is likely to be a seriously impaired communicator in both the oral and written mode. If the children are to be helped, it seems essential to obtain information for both understanding and treating this often-neglected component of language.

A Concluding Comment

A number of varied language factors have been raised in this presentation. Underlying all, however, is the concept of discourse. Each component that has been discussed can exist only within the context of a sustained exchange — whether it be in the oral or written mode. Since interest in discourse is relatively recent, this area of language is marked by limited understanding. Therefore, the present discussion is presented not as a definitive statement, but as a useful beginning for exploring the nature of the connections that exist between our two major systems of language.

References

BENTON, A.L., and PEARL, D. (1978) *Dyslexia: An Appraisal of Current Knowledge*, New York, Oxford University Press.

BLANK, M., and FRANKLIN, E. (1980) 'Dialogue with preschoolers: A cognitively-based system of assessment', *Applied Psycholinguistics*, 1, pp. 127–50.

BLANK, M., GESSNER, M., and ESPOSITO, A. (1979) 'Language without communication: A case study', *Journal of Child Language*, 6, pp. 329–52.

BLANK, M., ROSE, S.A., and BERLIN, L. (1978) *The Language of Learning: The Preschool Years*, New York, Grune and Stratton.

CLARK, R. (1980) Errors in talking to learn', *First Language*, 1, pp. 7–32.

DONALDSON, M. (1978) *Children's Minds*, New York, Norton.

EASTMAN, P.D. (1968) *The Best Nest*, New York, Random House.

GOODMAN, K.S. and GOODMAN, Y.M. (1977) 'Learning about psycholinguistic processes by analyzing oral reading', *Harvard Educational Review*, 47, pp. 317–33.

HUNT, K.W. (1977) 'Early and late blooming syntactic structures', in COOPER, C. and ODELL, L. (Eds), *Evaluating Writing: Describing, Measuring, Judging*, Urbana, Ill, National Council of Teachers of English.

ISAACS, S. (1930) *Intellectual Growth in Young Children*, London, Routledge and Kegan Paul.

MAKAR, B.W. (1977) *'The Wig' in Primary Phonics*, Cambridge, Mass, Educators Publishing Service.

MOFFETT, J. (1968) *Teaching the Universe of Discourse*, Boston, Houghton Mifflin.

UTTLEY, A. (1980) *Squirrel Goes Skating*, Great Britain, Collins Colour Cubs.

WALKER, C.H., and MEYER, B.J.F. (1980) 'Integrating information from text: An evaluation of current theories', *Review of Educational Research*, 50, pp. 421–37.

Part 2: Readiness and the Language of Reading

Introduction

Chapter 1 of a book by Downing entitled *Reading and Reasoning*, which was published in 1979, is the first paper in this section. Downing stresses the importance of taking account of the evidence over the past two decades from a variety of disciplines in any consideration of readiness for reading, and also in any attempt to understand reading disability. These findings he indicates are now 'fitting together' to reveal that a critical feature in developing reading skill is 'the child's clarity of thought in the reasoning and problem-solving tasks involved in learning how to read'. More recent evidence would perhaps lead some to challenge his use of the term 'cognitive confusion' to describe young children's state on entry to school as, active in learning about their environment, they form and test hypotheses about print. His emphasis on the cognitive aspects of the task fits well, however, with the views expressed in the previous section and is supported by extensive references from a number of countries.

Downing stresses the importance of appreciating that in learning to read there are two groups of concepts to be mastered: (a) functional concepts; and (b) featural concepts. His reference to the finding that backward readers may indeed be 'over-analytic' (as could be some beginning readers), possibly as a result of a lack of understanding of the critical features in the task, has important implications for methods of teaching reading and for the materials used. The need for children to apply reasoning abilities to understanding the linguistic relationship between speech and writing is explored further in the subsequent chapters of Downing's book from which the present extract is taken and by authors of the remaining chapters in this publication.

The two other papers in this section were written specifically for this publication, based on work undertaken while the authors were Master's level students of the editor. Both authors are practising teachers, Sutton is headteacher of a nursery school in which she undertook the study reported briefly here. van Lierop, who is in a multicultural education service, has based her paper on journal records of her daughter's early development which she analyzed retrospectively. Both authors were familiar with the work of the authors extracts from whose work are reprinted here. Sutton reports on a study of the awareness of print of a group of young children immediately prior to entry to reception class. A brief review of the various features which are reported in the literature as found in children who read early is followed by an outline of the range of functional and featural concepts she explored with the young children in her own school, none of whom were yet able to read. The major emphasis in her current paper is the aspect of her study within which she explored the children's developing awareness of story as they predicted subsequent phrases and outcomes using semantic and syntactic clues. The willingness of these young children to concentrate for long periods when their interest was captured, their abilities to share in the story development, their varied levels of competence in the different print-related features have important implications for initial literacy learning.

A study of published work on early reading led van Lierop to return to the journal records she had kept on her young daughter's early development as she became a 'young fluent reader' well before entry to school. In her report, as in those she cites as references, the importance of the interactive nature of the child's early experiences of print is apparent, as is the problem-solving nature of her early encounters with language, oral and written and with other media of communication.

As was noted earlier, Downing referred to both the importance of the problem-solving nature of the task of reading and to the functional and featural concepts which must be mastered. In the papers by Sutton and by van Lierop these aspects are explored empirically. The scene for this section is set by the reprinted chapter by Downing, followed in the two new papers by extensive reviews of recent publications as well as reference to some cited by Downing. van Lierop provides a detailed analysis of the functional and featural concepts learnt in the development literacy of a single child in a natural setting. Sutton, in contrast, shows the range of skills that are brought by young children to the task of learning to read and the wide individual differences in these.

In this section the focus is mainly on reading. In the following section attention will be directed to the productive aspect of literacy, writing, and its relationship to reading.

The Child's Understanding of the Functions and Processes of Communication★

John Downing

> If a man will begin with certainties, he shall end in doubts; but if he will be content to begin with doubts, he shall end in certainties. (Francis Bacon, *Advancement of Learning*, 1605.)

Our ignorance about how children learn to read is still enormous, despite all the research that has been carried out. Nevertheless, every now and again we make a small step forward by recognizing the importance of some key question in our theoretical understanding of reading. There are signs that we are now on the threshold of such an advance. In the past two decades a number of different researchers, in diverse countries and working on separate lines of enquiry, have produced findings which now seem to be fitting together into the beginnings of a new theory of how children learn to read. Work from five areas — child development, special education, educational psychology, psycholinguistics, and reading itself — seems to link up to indicate that the critical factor in developing reading skill may be the child's clarity of thought in the reasoning and problem-solving tasks involved in learning how to read. In this chapter we shall review the relevant research from psychology and education. This research review is designed to give the reader a picture of how various lines of investigation come together to support the 'cognitive clarity theory of learning to read'. 'Cognitive clarity' is used here as a technical label for the psychological components that lie behind what the layman might refer to as 'clear understanding', 'clear thinking', 'grasping the problem', or, even more colloquially, 'the penny dropping'.

We shall begin by studying the evidence that school beginners start out with only vague ideas about what goes on in communication either in speech or in writing. Then we shall turn to research on the causes of

★ Originally, published in DOWNING, J. (1979) *Reading and Reasoning*, London, Chambers.

reading disability that indicates that one of the main factors is a failure in logical reasoning that has been labelled 'cognitive confusion'. This will lead us to consider what are the main types of concept that the child must understand in order to succeed in reasoning about reading. The research suggests that there are two groups of concepts to be learned: (1) functional concepts (2) featural concepts. These will be described in turn in detail. All this research information is vital to understanding the cognitive clarity theory.

Child Language and Thought

The research component from the child-development field goes back much further than the past two decades. Piaget's (1959) *The Language and Thought of the Child* was first published in 1926. In that book the then revolutionary proposal was made that a surprisingly large proportion of the language of children younger than about eight years of age does not have the function of communication with others. This type of language Piaget called 'egocentric'. In egocentric talk, even if other children are present as an audience, the child 'does not attempt to place himself at the point of view of his hearer . . . He feels no desire to influence his hearer nor to tell him anything.' Piaget found that nearly half of children's language at the age of six years was egocentric. From about the age of 7, children 'try to improve upon their methods of interchanging ideas and upon their mutual understanding of one another', but Piaget emphasized that even then their success in communication is far from perfect.

Piaget's analysis of the functions of language was surprising to many who had assumed that communication was its sole function. Often his findings have produced an over-reaction, and the significance of the young child's language for social communication has been underestimated. Vygotsky (1962), perhaps sensing the danger of this over-reaction to Piaget's discovery, reasserted the communicative function of speech. He stressed that 'the primary function of speech, in both children and adults, is communication, social contact.' More recently, Halliday (1975) has shown that the very beginnings of language come from the child's problem-solving behaviour to serve evolving needs and developmental tasks. The child learns the language of his community as a by-product of striving for these other goals. Grammar is not learned by some mysterious instinctive process, as Chomsky seems to think. Grammar in Halliday's view is learned because it is a functional necessity for the child. Grammar increases the child's scope for communication.

Halliday distinguishes between 'pragmatic' and 'mathetic' functions of speech. The pragmatic functions are the intrusive, interactive and manipulative aspects of speech. The mathetic functions consist in declarative and observational utterances that occur when the child attempts to understand the self and the surrounding world. These mathetic functions are especially important for us because they lead the child to become aware of language itself.

Halliday's theory and research is of great potential interest to specialists in reading education. Learning to read is only one aspect of the development of 'a language for life'. The acquisition of reading skill is an integral part of this total development. Halliday provides a functional analysis of language development that indicates the continuity of the process. Literacy extends the scope of the pragmatic functions of language, and learning how to read and write is a natural extension of the mathetic functions, as the child increases his own understanding of the functions and features of language.

At the typical age for beginning school, the child is very limited in his communication experiences. Indeed, as Piaget showed, children's communication skills may often be retarded because parents appear to read their children's thoughts in fulfilling their wishes without being asked verbally.

Piaget demonstrated the young child's ineffectiveness in communication in a series of experiments in which the experimenter explained a simple object to one child who then had to explain it to a second child. The results were revealing. Communication broke down because, firstly, the explaining child did not appreciate that his hearer knew less than he did, and, secondly, because the hearer did not recognize that the explainer possessed more information than he had. Both were egocentric in failing to take account of the other child's point of view. Piaget commented that adults, in contrast, usually 'make an effort to understand and be understood . . ., because experience has shown them the appalling density of the human mind. Children have no suspicion of all this. They think that they both understand and are understood.'

More recently, Krauss and Glucksberg (1969) gave children at four grade levels (kindergarten and grades one, three and five) a task in which they had to communicate a description of novel graphic designs to a partner of the same age. Grade three and grade five pupils improved rapidly at the task. Grade one children showed much less improvement, and kindergarten pupils showed no progress at all.

The important point from this line of inquiry is that the typical school beginner arrives with poor communication skills and that the cause of this is his lack of awareness of the communication process. The school beginner has not perceived communication as a problem. He has not thought about its functions or techniques. Therefore, he lacks functional or technical concepts of elements of communication through spoken language. Since the pre-school child's experience with written language is more limited than with speech, we would anticipate very little awareness of the functions of writing. This was confirmed by Vygotsky's (1962) finding that the school beginner 'has little motivation to learn writing when we begin to teach it. He feels no need for it and has only a vague idea of its usefulness.' Vygotsky's choice of words is notable. The child has 'a vague idea' of the communication functions of written language, just as he has only vague conceptions of the communication process in general.

Cognitive Confusion

The second area of investigation that provides evidence for the cognitive clarity theory of learning to read is the study of children who have failed in reading. Vernon (1957) reviewed all the related research on the causes of reading disability. She concluded that 'the fundamental and basic characteristic of reading disability appears to be cognitive confusion and lack of system . . . It must be attributed to a failure in analyzing, abstraction and generalization, but one which, typically, is confined to linguistics.' Vernon said that 'the fundamental trouble appears to be a failure in development of this reasoning process.' She described the cognitively confused child as being 'hopelessly uncertain and confused as to why certain successions of printed letters should correspond to certain phonetic sounds in words'. In her more recent extension of her survey of research on reading disability, Vernon (1971) develops this theme further:

> It would seem that in learning to read it is essential for the child to realize and understand the fundamental generalization that in alphabetic writing all words are represented by combinations of a limited number of visual symbols. Thus it is possible to present a very large vocabulary of spoken words in an economical manner which requires the memorizing of a comparatively small number of printed symbols and their associated sounds. But a thorough grasp of this principle necessitates a fairly advanced stage of conceptual reasoning, since this type of organization differs fundamentally from any previously encountered by children in their normal environment.

With regard to simple associationistic views of learning the letter/sound code, Vernon asserts:

> The employment of reasoning is almost certainly involved in understanding the variable associations between printed and sounded letters. It might appear that certain writers suppose that these associations may be acquired through rote learning. But even if this is possible with very simple letter-phoneme associations, the more complex associations and the correct application of the rules of spelling necessitate intelligent comprehension.

Vernon's emphasis on failure in the processes of reasoning and understanding as the key factor in reading disability seems to be supported by several other independent observations. Serafica and Sigel (1970) compared a group of reading-disabled boys with a group of similar boys, also in grades two to four, who were normal readers. They reported that the boys with reading disability were 'better equipped' for 'differentiation of graphic symbols' than were the normal readers. What is most interesting in the study of Serafica and Sigel is that the superior analytical ability of the disabled readers was at the expense of the conceptual process of categorizing. Other evidence supports the interpretation that these disabled readers were probably failing *because* they were over-analytic and this was due to their lack of understanding of the task. They probably did not know how to sort the relevant cues from the irrelevant details. Robinson (1953) cites a study by Solomon in which an association was found between reading disability and a general personality trait of preoccupation with unimportant details. There are many variations both in print and speech which must be ignored because they are irrelevant in the code. Klapper (1968) notes that disabled readers frequently have difficulty in categorizing graphic symbols which vary in shape, size and spatial position.

The insight gained from these studies of reading disability is that learning to read is essentially a problem-solving task in which the child applies reasoning abilities to understanding the linguistic relationships between speech and writing. Cognitive confusion is the chief symptom of reading disability, according to Vernon. Therefore, if we generalize from her finding, we may postulate that cognitive clarity should be the typical characteristic of the successful reader. He or she will be a pupil who brings clear thinking to the task of reasoning about what to do in learning how to read and write.

Reasoning About Reading

It is often asserted that reading difficulties are related to maldevelopment of visual perceptual abilities. For example, it is still popular to cite children's confusion between letters *b* and *d* as a symptom of faulty visual perception associated with developmental dyslexia. But such notions are derived from outmoded psychological theories of perception. No modern theory would assume such a passive role for the eye, which is in fact an active extension of a reasoning brain. As Piaget (1969) points out:

> The subject does not submit himself to the constraints of the object but directs his perceptual activities as if he were solving a problem . . . What is more remarkable is the number of steps involved in making even the most elementary estimation, such as size; far from remaining simply receptive, the subject proceeds by a method of sampling, selecting the most profitable point of concentration, hoping to multiply encounters and co-ordinate them by an exercise of couplings.

The importance of reasoning in the perceptual activities involved in learning to read seems to be suggested when Piaget continues: 'When it becomes a question of the identification of objects even more complex activities are required.'

The problem of identifying the objects *b* and *d* is that these letters contradict most of the child's previous experience in object identification — that is that an object remains the same object in spite of differences in its orientation. Hence, mistaking *b* for *d* from the viewpoint of the school beginner is not an error. All his previous experience has taught him that orientation is irrelevant. A chair is still a chair no matter what direction it faces, for example. When introduced to reading, however, the child must solve the problem that, unexpectedly, orientation makes a difference and he must remember which orientation of a lettershape is logically related to which phoneme. This is just one example of the importance of reasoning in the learning to read process.

One of the most exciting areas of research on the psychology of learning to read in the past decade has been in exploring how children think about reading, how they puzzle out what adults do when they read, and what their parents and teachers mean in their talk about language, speech, writing, print and books. This is what Fitts and Posner (1967) describe as the 'cognitive phase' that is characteristically the initial phase of all skill learning. The beginner must find out, firstly, the functions or purposes of the skilled act and its component sub-skills, and secondly, he must understand the technical concepts needed for thinking about the linguistic features involved in the task of developing the skill. The next section of this chapter describes the functional concepts. The concepts of linguistic features will be described in Chapter 2.

Functional Concepts of Literacy

For more than thirty years, Piaget's finding that children of the typical age for beginning school have little awareness of the functions of communication, and Vygotsky's comment that young beginners have 'only a vague idea' of the 'usefulness' of writing, received very little attention from reading specialists. Then the practical significance of the theories of these two child psychologists was made clear by an investigation conducted by Reid (1966) in Scotland. She made an intensive study of twelve 5-year-olds at a school in Edinburgh. Her article, 'Learning to think about reading', describes how these children's conceptions of reading and language developed during their first year of schooling. Reid found that they all began with a general lack of any idea 'of the purpose and use of [written language]'. Reid's investigation was replicated with a group of children in England and substantially the same results were obtained, leading to the conclusion that 'young beginners have difficulty in understanding the *purpose* of written language' (Downing, 1970).

Subsequently, Evanechko *et al.* (1973) developed a battery of reading readiness tests including a new 'Orientation to Literacy Test' that measures the child's understanding of the simplest concepts of the communication functions of literacy. This test has been employed to find out how the development of these concepts is related to the child's experiences. In the first investigation (Downing, Ollila and Oliver, 1975), two groups of Canadian Indian beginners were found to be significantly less aware of the purposes of reading and writing than were non-Indian beginners attending the kindergarten classes in the same school districts. This supported the hypothesis that the Indian children's concepts of the functions of writing are less well-developed because they come from a home background with no cultural tradition of literacy. In a second study (Downing, Ollila and Oliver, 1977), it was found that children from lower socio-economic levels of the population in a Canadian city began school with significantly less understanding of the functions of writing than children from higher socio-economic levels of the population in the same city. These two studies indicate that experience at home is an important factor in learning the purposes of reading and writing.

To an adult this problem may seem so simple that it is hardly worth troubling about. Yet the research evidence leads to a quite contrary conclusion. Understanding of the functions of reading and writing is of crucial importance and it is not acquired easily. Probably the most important single fact about the process of reading is that the purpose of the reading act is inextricably interwoven in its technique. In other words, the ends are an integral part of the means. Again, some initial clues to this important characteristic of reading were given to us by early investigators. Thorndike's (1917) research on reading comprehension led him to conclude: 'The mind is assailed as it were by every word in the paragraph. It must select, repress, soften, emphasize, correlate and organize, all under the influence of the right mental set or purpose or demand.' An indication of the key significance of purpose in reading was also given by two other classical studies. Both Gray (1917) and Judd and Buswell (1922) found that eye movements in reading change according to the purpose.

On this matter too, it took several decades before these important early findings were followed up and applied. In recent years, studies in psycholinguistics have shown how the reader's purpose influences the process of comprehension. For example, Postman and Senders (1946) showed by experiment that college students' reading comprehension was significantly influenced by the purpose they were instructed to adopt. Furthermore, purpose influences reading strategy, whether it is stated or not. Russell (1970) concluded: 'The dominant factor in comprehension, accordingly, is the purpose of the reader, stated or unstated.' Indeed, Rickards and August (1975) found that college students 'who were free to underline any one sentence per paragraph recalled significantly more incidental material than those explicitly instructed to underline the one sentence per paragraph that was most important to the overall meaning of each paragraph.' The Rickards and August study suggests that setting one's own purpose may bring the highest returns in comprehension. As Bond and Tinker (1973) have put it: 'To be a really good reader . . . the pupil must have learned to set his own purpose.'

Different purposes require different reading techniques. Therefore, Burmeister (1974) states that secondary school pupils need to learn to 'use different rates for various types of materials and/or when reading for different purposes.' Russell also concluded that 'one of the most important reading heights we can gain is that of flexibility of reading in different ways for different purposes.'

Unfortunately, two road-blocks have hindered the proper application of these important research findings in the schools. Firstly, administrators have failed to recognize that secondary schools have an important role in developing higher levels of reading skill. Secondly, practices in the elementary stage of education quite often are not well co-ordinated with the comprehension needs of subject-matter reading assignments in high schools and colleges. These are world-wide problems of key importance in raising functional literacy standards. This is why Bond and Tinker can report: 'Too many students at all grade levels, even in high school and college, tend to read everything at approximately the same rate irrespective of the kind of material or the purpose for reading it.'

One of the main causes of this inflexibility and lack of purpose in older students' reading is the narrowness of teaching methods and reading experiences at the primary level. Furthermore, the focus often tends to be on the rote learning of technical relations between letters and sounds and printed and spoken words, with little attention to developing an understanding of the communication process and the functions of writing and reading. However, the Bullock Report shows a keen awareness of the need for purpose to be integrated with skill development in the beginning and continuously thereafter. Two quotations typical of the Bullock Report's consistent theme are:

> Competence in language comes above all through its purposeful use, not through the working of exercises divorced from context. . . .
>
> Language development . . . involves creating situations in which, to satisfy his own purposes, a child encounters the need to use more elaborate forms and is thus motivated to extend the complexity of language available to him.

These recommendations are cognisant of the principle that concepts are learned from experience with their exemplars. Therefore, teaching an understanding of the functions of written language requires the provision of experiences with reading and writing activities that are purposeful for the individual. The Bullock Report recommends that more deliberate instruction in the communicative function of written language should be provided as the pupil's conception of purpose develops. For example, it states that: 'If a child knows that what he is writing is going to interest and entertain others, he will be more careful with its presentation.' Also, 'The child should not be made to feel that it does not pay to take risks. If a pupil is progressively to develop control in his handling of language he needs opportunity to experiment with new forms, and to do so with security.' Therefore there should be more use of 'the idea of a first draft to be followed by a second more refined production. Merely to assign a grade to every piece of writing works against the notion of writing as communication.' It is important to note also that the Bullock Report treats reading and writing as two of the several integrated aspects of developing 'a language for life'.

A successful application of these principles has been seen in many schools using the language-experience approach to reading. Particularly effective have been the programmes developed under the leadership of Harry Hahn at Oakland University in Michigan. Several years ago he introduced the idea of 'young authors' conferences'. At these meetings, children from schools in an area meet with each other and with adult authors of published children's books to confer about the techniques and purposes of creative writing. In a similar vein, the Bullock Commission notes: 'The novel features in the task and the language it demands can be explored in discussion with the individual or the group, and supporting examples collected and worked upon. The child should thus be led to greater control over his writing, with a growing knowledge of how to vary its effects.'

One investigation that shows the relationship between children's understanding of the functions of literacy and their attainments in reading is that by Clay (1976) in New Zealand. She compared three cultural groups: (1) 'Pakehas' — the majority white population; (2) the native Maoris; (3) immigrants from the Pacific Islands — notably Western Samoans. She found that the Samoans made better progress in learning to read in the early years than did the Maoris. This was shown to be related to the Samoan child's superior understanding of the purposes of literacy. This better understanding was derived from frequent experiences of being read to from the Bible, and from observing the high value placed on written communication between their parents and relatives in the home country. The Maori children in contrast did not have such experiences.

A rather different approach to developing awareness of the process and functions of communication is currently being worked out in the USSR, in an experimental school in Moscow. The writer observed these experiments on a recent visit to Professor Elkonin in the Academy of Pedagogical Sciences of the USSR. In the primary classes a new system of symbols is being created that provides a code for a functional description of the relations between thought, speech, and writing. Children use this code for analyzing problems of communication, individually and in class discussion.

Thus, in various ways and in various places, research, experiment and creative teaching are focusing on the importance of the child's reasoning about, and understanding of, the functions of communication in writing and reading.

References

BOND, G.L. and TINKER, M.A. (1973) *Reading Difficulties: their Diagnosis and Correction*, (3rd edn.), New York, Appleton-Century-Crofts.

Bullock Report, see Department of Education and Science.

BURMEISTER, L.E. (1974) *Reading Strategies for Secondary School Teachers*, Reading, Mass, Addison-Wesley.

CLAY, M.M. (1976) 'Early childhood and cultural diversity in New Zealand,' *Reading Teacher*, 29, pp. 333–42.

DEPARTMENT OF EDUCATION AND SCIENCE (1975) *A Language for Life*, (The Bullock Report), London, HMSO.

DOWNING, J. (1970) 'Children's concepts of language in learning to read,' *Educational Research*, 12, pp. 106–12.

DOWNING, J., OLLILA, L. and OLIVER, P. (1975) 'Cultural differences in children's concepts of reading and writing,' *British Journal of Educational Psychology*, 45, pp. 312–16.

DOWNING, J., OLLILA, L. and OLIVER, P. (1977) 'Concepts of language in children from differing socio-economic backgrounds,' *Journal of Educational Research*, 70, pp. 277–81.

EVANECHKO, P., OLLILA, L., DOWNING, J. and BRAUN, C. (1973) 'An investigation of the reading readiness domain', *Research in the Teaching of English*, 7, pp. 61–78.

FITTS, P.M. and POSNER, M.I. (1967) *Human Performance*, Belmont, Calif., Brooks-Cole.

GRAY, C.T. (1917) 'Types of reading ability as exhibited through tests and laboratory experiments', *Supplementary Educational Monographs No. 5*, University of Chicago Press.

HALLIDAY, M.A.K. (1975) *Learning How to Mean*, London, Edward Arnold.

JUDD. C.H. and BUSWELL, G. (1922) 'Silent reading: a study of the various types', *Supplementary Educational Monographs No. 23*, University of Chicago Press.

KLAPPER, Z.S. (1968) 'Psychological aspects of reading disabilities', in NATCHEZ, G. (Ed.) *Children with Reading Problems*, New York, Basic Books.

KRAUSS, R.M. and GLUCKSBERG, S. (1969) 'The development of communication competence as a function of age', *Child Development*, 40, pp. 255–66.

PIAGET, J. (1959) *The Language and Thought of the Child*, London, Routledge and Kegan Paul.

PIAGET, J. (1969) *The Mechanisms of Perception*, London, Routledge and Kegan Paul.

POSTMAN, L. and SENDERS, V. (1946) 'Incidental learning and generality of set', *Journal of Experimental Psychology*, 36, pp. 153–65.

REID, J.F. (1966) 'Learning to think about reading, *Educational Research*, 9, pp. 56–62.

RICKARDS, J.P. and AUGUST, G.J. (1975) 'Generative underlining strategies in prose recall', *Journal of Educational Psychology*, 67, pp. 860–5.

ROBINSON, H.M. (1953) 'Diagnosis and treatment of poor readers with vision

problems', *Clinical Studies in Reading, II (Supplementary Educational Monographs No. 77). University of Chicago Press.*
RUSSELL, D.H. (1970) *The Dynamics of Reading*, Waltham, Mass, Ginn-Blaisdell.
SERAFICA, F.C. and SIGEL, I.E. (1970) 'Styles of categorization and reading disability', *Journal of Reading Behavior*, 2, pp. 105–15.
THORNDIKE, E.L. (1917) 'Reading as reasoning; a study of mistakes in paragraph reading', *Journal of Educational Psychology*, 8, pp. 323–32.
VERNON, M.D. (1957) *Backwardness in Reading*, London, Cambridge University Press.
VERNON, M.D. (1971) *Reading and Its Difficulties*, Cambridge University Press.
VYGOTSKY, L.S. (1962) *Thought and Language*, Cambridge, Mass, MIT Press.

Some Factors in Pre-school Children of Relevance to Learning to Read

Wendy Sutton

In the previous article, Downing observed that, over the past two decades, research from the separate fields of child development, special education, educational psychology, psycholinguistics and reading has produced findings which could combine to contribute to a new theory of how children learn to read. He indicated that recent research in many countries has focused on the fundamental importance of children's ability to understand and to reason about the communicative functions of reading and writing. The early development of this ability has been identified, with a number of other factors, in several studies of children who read before school.

Summary of Factors Identified from Previous Research as Relevant to Early Reading

When considering ways in which reception class teachers can best approach the early stages of the teaching of reading, it is worth summarizing the personal qualities, abilities and environmental factors which are currently considered to be relevant to the process of learning to read (that is, those most often identified in studies of early, or 'natural' readers).

1 Summary of Personal Qualities Observed in Studies of Early Readers

Children were said (by parents and teachers) to be
(a) curious and questioning;
(b) conscientious;
(c) serious-minded; (Durkin, 1961)
(d) persistent;

(e) self-reliant;
(f) self-sufficient. (Clark, 1976)

2 Summary of Skills and Abilities

(a) Children had the ability to concentrate for long periods (observed by parents and teachers) (Durkin, 1961; Clark, 1976).
(b) They had exceptionally good memories (Durkin, 1961); auditory memory was found to be particularly strong (Clark, 1976), as was visual memory (Lass, 1983).
(c) Their linguistic development was precocious, in terms of advanced oral language skills, combined with the ability and confidence to respond well in adult/child interactions, including contrived or test situations (Clark, 1976).

Although the mean IQ scores of early readers was above average and some individual children had very high scores, a wide range of scores was recorded, indicating that not all early readers are highly intelligent according to conventional IQ tests and that a high intelligence quotient *per se* is not a necessary condition for early reading development (Durkin, 1961; Clark, 1976; Lass, 1983).

3 Summary of Environmental and Social Factors

(a) Children were strongly motivated to read. The motivation was functional; they read for pleasure or specific information (Clark, 1976). Their perception about what reading 'means' probably affected their attitude to and therefore success at it (Durkin, 1961).
(b) Children showed an early interest in environmental print, including print on television; this was an interest apparently not always initiated by their parents (Clark, 1976; Goodman, 1982; Lass, 1983).
(c) Children's families appeared to have a high regard for reading (Durkin, 1961). Library membership, regular library visits and help with choice of books, together with a more general enthusiasm about and interest in all their children did, typified the parents of early readers (Clark, 1976 and 1982).
(d) At least one person at home (parent or sibling) was willing to answer children's 'constant' questions about words and reading (Durkin, 1961), probably answering in particular those questions most relevant to learning to read (Torrey, 1973), and answering questions about, not only print, but the child's world in general (Clark, 1976; Lass, 1983).
(e) Homes showed evidence of books and educational toys (Lass, 1983).

(f) When observed by teachers at school, the early readers seemed to have adjusted happily to the situation and were well integrated with their classmates (Clark, 1976).

Other qualities and skills, not necessarily observed in studies of self-taught early readers, have been considered relevant to reading by some past and many present authorities on reading:

(a) the enjoyment of stories through frequent repetition (Huey, 1908) and subsequently the understanding and assimilation of story schema (Teale, 1982);
(b) the awareness of the relationship and at the same time the differences between conversation and spoken prose (for example, story language), subsequently written prose (Marquardt, 1964; Smith, 1971; Johnson, 1977; Goodman, 1982; Francis, 1982);
(c) the 'fundamental insight' that print is meaningful (Smith, 1971) and the active endeavour to ascertain meaning (Payton, 1982);
(d) the understanding that it is the print which conveys meaning in a book, of how to handle a book, holding it right way up and turning the pages, and the left to right directionality of print (all 'concepts of print') (Clay, 1979; Goodman, 1982).
(e) the ability to sample cues, both visual and contextual, to form hypotheses and make predictions which are confirmed or otherwise by subsequent sampling (Levin and Williams, 1970; Smith, 1971; Clay, 1979).
(f) the necessity of a high level of response, for example so that errors and self-correction can be observed (Clay, 1969 and 1979; Bissex, 1982).

As this summary of the factors considered relevant to learning to read has been based mainly on research involving children who read before school, it may be useful to look at the results of a study which involved pre-school children not yet able to read, and to consider the extent to which these children already possessed or had begun to develop abilities and skills which could provide a starting point for their introduction to the reading process.

Twenty nursery school children were selected for the study (Sutton, 1984), of whom ten were girls and ten boys. Their ages were between 4 years 5 months and 4 years 9 months. All had full-time nursery places, had been at nursery school for roughly the same length of time and constituted the group of children due to transfer to infant reception classes in September 1983. The local authority nursery school from which all the children were drawn is situated on the outskirts of a large industrial city; its intake is mainly from a nearby housing estate (small, three-bedroomed, first-time-buyer property). Most of the children are white, native English speakers, with young parents and not more than one or two siblings. Fathers are mostly, but not all, skilled workers, and unemployment in the area has become rather high in recent years. For the purposes of this research, no ethnic minority children were selected, no children previously identified as having 'special needs' (linguistic, or other) and no children from single parent families or known to have serious social problems.

The Range of Assessments, Involving Children, Parents and Teachers

It has become increasingly difficult to justify the application of standardized tests to young children in the hope of deciding whether the children are 'ready' to begin the formal process of reading. Teachers need to consider whether it is best to put all children on to the same formal pre-reading and reading programme as soon as they start school, or whether there may be a range of relevant observations and assessments, albeit producing highly individual results, which should be used to determine each child's starting point, in terms of, for example, extending experience, involving parents and stimulating interest by the selection of subject matter.

For the purposes of this study, therefore, tests, questions and interviews were selected which, it was hoped, would sample the level of those factors amenable to such quantification in the group of young children (who had received no formal reading instruction and of whom none had begun to read at the time of the research).

Most of the assessments are described briefly here; the Probe Analysis (Lewis, 1982), however, is a comparatively new way of sampling certain aspects of children's understanding of the functions of reading and writing and is therefore examined in more detail.

1 Pre-school Language Assessment Instrument (Blank, Rose and Berlin, 1978)

This test was designed to give a profile of pre-school children's discourse skills. There are sixty questions, fifteen at each of four levels of complexity, yet requiring limited language in response. This assessment, the probe analysis and the interviews with children and their nursery teacher took place during the children's last term at nursery school, in July 1983.

2 Child Interview

(i) Concepts of print (from *Reading: The Patterning of Complex Behaviour* (Clay, 1972))

This section was based on observations by Clay about beginning readers' developing concepts of print, including the awareness that the direction of reading (at any rate in English) is from left to right and from top to bottom of the page.

(ii) Discrimination of letters and numbers, discrimination of terms 'letter', 'word' and 'sentence', and reading questionnaire (from *Learning to Read: Literate Behaviour and Orthographic Knowledge*, (Francis, 1982))

These were the tests used by Francis on 5-year-old beginning readers; only the first part of her questionnaire was considered relevant for pre-readers.

3 *Nursery Teacher's Comments*

The teacher's comments were invited about the children's enjoyment of stories at school, their relationship with adults and peers and their preferred activities.

4 *Parental Interview* (from *Young Fluent Readers* (Clark, 1976))

The questions were based on those used by Clark, excluding questions which related specifically to established reading ability, and adapting some of the questions she used about parental help with fluent readers' self-taught skills so that they could be asked of parents who were helping their children with their first school-based reading efforts.

5 *Infant Teacher Questions*

Although the observations of the infant staff had limited value, in that the children had been with them for less than three months and little that was conclusive could be said about their early reading progress, it was possible to obtain some information relating to the children's first experiences of formal reading instruction. The interviews with parents and reception class teachers took place during the children's first term at infant school (autumn 1983).

6 *Probe Analysis* (from *Children's perception of dynamics in narrative prose* (Lewis, 1983)

Lewis' work with remedial readers led him to the observation that texts devised for children with reading difficulties, which tend to consist of simple words, short sentences and frequent repetition, are not 'natural' and not sufficiently dynamic for their purpose of motivating children already discouraged by failure. He examined reading process models, comparing 'bottom-up' theories (those which generate schemes based on the smallest units of language initially, i.e. letters and words, and in which meaning is not important in the early stages) with 'top-down' theories (whose proponents regard reading as prediction or guessing, in which meaning is predominant from the beginning). He concluded that neither theory could completely account for the complex process of reading and that an interactive model provides a more satisfactory explanation, allowing as it does for different readers to bring different knowledge, experience and strategies to the reading process. He criticized the texts used in conventional reading assessment, many of which consist of word lists, sentence completion, cloze procedure, comprehension questions, or miscue analysis, advocating instead a test which would consist of a 'natural' text or exposition, with a way of interrupting it at certain points to sample children's textual understanding and predictive skills.

He selected a suitable children's story (i.e. one with a setting and involving a number of characters; see Rumelhart, (1975) *Notes on a Schema for Stories*). The story chosen was *The Giant's Socks* (almost 600 words in length), written by Ben Butterworth and published by E.J. Arnold. Ten 8-year-old readers were originally tested. They were asked to read the story (silently, if they wished), then stopped at nineteen pre-determined points beyond which the text had been concealed and asked to predict, 'What comes next?', a question which permitted a response at a number of levels from the readers. Probes were inserted at points deemed interesting or significant in the text. Two types of probe were used (based on categories of Probing and Detection developed by Shine in 1975). The standard probe required a single response, although this response could range from a word to a number of sentences, depending on the individual reader. The rolling probe involved revealing subsequent text, one word at a time, to show ways in which predictions were maintained or altered during the course of reading. Lewis recognized that the reading task was inevitably distorted by the interruption of the process brought about by the probe response elicitation, but believed that the use of a complete natural text of narrative prose, thus enabling full 'use of context' by readers, was likely to produce a more realistic result than most standard tests.

Although this probe analysis was designed for use with 8-year-old readers, it was considered feasible to adapt it for use with 4-year-old pre-readers. A number of changes were made, but the story itself was retained. Although in some ways a complex and even sophisticated story, with an unexpected twist at the end, it was considered, in terms of length, interest, syntax and lexis, a comprehensible story for nursery age children.

The story was read to each individual child by the tester. It was hoped that intonation, rather than visually presented punctuation, would provide clues to prediction. It could even be argued that to read a story to a child (having first explained that the reader would like the child to help in the telling of the story) and to stop at probe points, using a rising intonation and looking expectantly at the child, comprises a more natural interruption than concealing text, stopping and asking, 'What comes next?'.

Each of the children sat close enough to the tester to see the print and the pages being turned. The text took the form of a booklet, with short pages of print and no illustrations, exactly similar to that presented to Lewis' readers. The story was read twice. Eleven new probes replaced the nineteen original ones for the first reading, selected for their simplicity and lack of ambiguity. These probes were designed to elicit a very basic response but, like Lewis' original probes, were inserted at points considered interesting or significant; rolling probes were not used during the first reading. When the story was read for the second time (immediately following the first), each child was asked to help tell the story again. Lewis' original probes, considered too complex for the first reading, were used for the second; children's responses to both readings were recorded.

It was hoped that probe analysis would provide evidence of the children's understanding of and ability to use story language and a story schema (i.e. their concept of 'storyness') and that it would sample their predictive skills and willingness to take risks when making predictions. As the story was repeated and some of the probes were common to both readings, or designed to elicit similar responses, short-term auditory memory was also effectively tested. Two readings of a fairly long story, without the additional information or attention holding function of illustrations, provided an incidental test of concentration.

The results of the assessments indicated a wide range of relevant abilities in the group tested. The children coped well with the Language Assessment Instrument; most of them were able to understand and use language fairly competently at four levels of complexity, with somewhat decreasing ability at the third and fourth levels.

Concepts of print had begun to develop, although the children's discrimination of letters, words and sentences and the ability to recognize specific examples of them were, as yet, not well-developed. The interviews with children revealed that most of them had clearly defined and 'motivating' reasons for wanting to be able to read; like Clark's (1976) *Young Fluent Readers*, their reasons were many and varied.

A particularly important aspect of the Parental Interview responses was the strong interest which all parents, without exception, expressed in their children's reading progress. This was regardless of the parents' own educational achievements or occupations (ranging from unemployed and unskilled, having left school at 16 with no formal qualifications to degree holders who had entered professions such as teaching). While all parents recognized the importance of their children's learning to read and were prepared to give time to helping them, some were unsure as to how best to help and indicated that they would have welcomed specific guidance from infant staff.

Probe analysis provided considerable evidence of the understanding and ability of most of the children to use story language and of their concept of story-ness, realized through predictions in response to a variety of probes. There are certain limitations in the use of probe analysis. It samples predictions made by children at a particular moment in time and a particular point in the revelation of narrative text; these predictions may differ from those constantly being made by readers in their interaction with text. The strengths of probe analysis are its facility for sampling the individual ways of interacting with the language of narrative text and its recognition that reading (in this case, listening to) a story is an active process, involving productive, as well as receptive language skills. A number of interesting results emerged from this use of probe analysis with pre-reading children.

(a) All the children, with no exceptions, appeared amused and interested throughout two readings of the story. Concentration, therefore, did not present a problem. Clearly, children can respond at a variety of levels to story; this would be untrue of most types of assessment, particularly those assigning a less active role to children.
(b) Most children produced predictions in the form of plausible word strings (which fulfilled the role of theme/rheme (Daneš, (1982) in Lewis).
(c) Many responses showed considerable flexibility, moving between a variety of semantic and syntactic features.
(d) Many predictions were dynamic, in that they maintained the story and moved it on.
(e) Some children's responses were more relevant to the story, being integrated with previously raised features.
(f) Surface structures, in this case realized by intonation patterns, were often ignored (cf Lewis' findings where punctuation was ignored), perhaps where children's pursuit of the story-line as they understood it ran counter to these structures.

Implications for Teachers of this Study

It is interesting that, across this group of children of similar age and pre-school experience, a wide range of abilities existed (probably reflecting very different home experiences as well as inherent differences). Of particular interest is the observation that the narrowest variation of ability appeared to exist in the children's response to probe analysis, which all twenty enjoyed and coped with well.

(i) Ability to Concentrate

Young children are often considered to have poorly developed concentration skills. The probe analysis assessment took about half an hour to administer and, as indicated, all twenty children concentrated throughout. It should be remembered that these children were not likely (due to the method of their selection and the geographical area from which the sample was drawn) to represent a group of above average ability. Their level of concentration in this situation may relate to their active involvement in a task which had interest and relevance for them.

(ii) Ability to Predict

Many of the children displayed confidence and adventurousness in their predictions, moving the story along in a dynamic way, while still keeping options open and maintaining the story-line. They were using semantic/syntactic clues in their predictions, not the visual/phonic clues which are used, sometimes without sufficient reference to meaning, by beginning readers. The children's understanding of a simple story schema and their ability to comprehend and use story language (their storyness) were well developed. These may be seriously underestimated abilities in young children, abilities which have clearly begun to develop before school age and which need to be taken into account by those teaching reading. Teachers should continue to be aware of the importance to young children of stories and other written forms; the introduction of a variety of these could help to further children's understanding of the communicative functions of reading and writing.

(iii) Parental Interest

If the interest of parents in their children's learning is as strong as this study suggests, then it would seem wasteful of a valuable teaching aid, to put it at its weakest, if teachers did not take advantage of this interest and involve parents in their children's reading activities in a far more positive way. To put it more strongly, it is hard to see how teachers can develop in children a real and lasting interest in books, without parental support. Most parents appear to believe in the superior knowledge of their children's teachers about the reading process and would welcome guidance on how to offer the most effective help.

References

*BISSEX, G. (1982) 'The child as teacher', paper presented at University of Victoria

Symposium, *Literacy Before Schooling* (unpublished).

BLANK, M., ROSE, S.A. and BERLIN, L.J. (1978) *The Language of Learning – The Pre-school Years* New York, Grune and Stratton.

CLARK, M.M. (1976) *Young Fluent Readers*, London, Heinemann.

CLARK, M.M. (1982) 'Language, communication and learning in the classroom', in WHELDALL, K. and RIDING, R.J. (Eds) *Psychological Aspects of Learning and Teaching*.

CLAY, M.M. (1969) 'Reading errors and self-correction behaviour', *British Journal of Educational Psychology*, 39, pp. 47–56.

CLAY, M.M. (1972) *Reading: The Patterning of Complex Behaviour*, Auckland, Heinemann.

DANEŠ, F. (1974) 'Functional sentence perspective and the organization of the text', in DANEŠ, F. (Ed.) *Papers on FSP* Prague, Academia.

DOWNING, J. (1979) *Reading and Reasoning*, London, Chambers.

DURKIN, D. (1961) 'Children who read before Grade I', *The Reading Teacher*, 14, pp. 163–6.

FRANCIS, H. (1982) *Learning to Read: Literate Behaviour and Orthographic Knowledge*, London, Allen and Unwin.

*GOODMAN, Y. (1982) 'Initial literacy', paper presented at University of Victoria Symposium, *Literacy Before Schooling* (unpublished).

HUEY, E.B. (1908) *The Psychology and Pedagogy of Reading*, Cambridge, Mass, MIT Press (reissued 1968).

JOHNSON, T.D. (1977) 'Language experience: we can't all write what we can say', *The Reading Teacher*, 31, pp. 297–9.

LASS, B. (1983) 'Portrait of my son as an early reader', *The Reading Teacher*, 35, pp. 20–8.

LEVIN, H. and WILLIAMS, J. (Eds) (1970) *Basic Studies on Reading*, New York, Basic Books.

LEWIS, G. (1982) 'Text structure, text processing and testing reading', *Midland Association for Linguistic Studies Journal*, 7, pp. 43–69.

LEWIS, G. (1983) 'Children's perception of dynamics in narrative prose', *Midland Association for Linguistic Studies Journal*, 8, pp. 31–46.

MARQUARDT, W. (1964) 'Language interference in reading', *The Reading Teacher*, Vol. 18.

*PAYTON, S. (1982) *Readiness for Reading as an Aspect of Language Growth*, MEd. dissertation, University of Birmingham (unpublished).

RUMELHART, D.E. (1975) 'Notes on a schema for stories', in BOBROW, D.G. and COLLINS, A. (Eds) *Representation and understanding: Studies in Cognitive Science*, New York, Academic Press.

SMITH, F. (1971) *Understanding Reading*, New York, Holt, Rinehart and Winston.

SUTTON, W.M. (1984) *The Assessment of Readiness for Reading*, MEd. dissertation, University of Birmingham (unpublished).

*TEALE, N.H. (1982) 'Reading to pre-school children; its significance in the process of literacy development', paper presented at University of Victoria Symposium, *Literacy Before Schooling* (unpublished).

TORREY, J.W. (1973) 'Learning to read without a teacher', in SMITH, F. (Ed.) *Psycholinguistics and Reading*, New York, Holt, Rinehart and Winston.

*These papers have now appeared in revised form in the following: GOELMAN, H., OBERG, A. and SMITH, F. (Eds) (1984) *Awakening to Literacy*, London, Heinemann Educational.

**A revised version of this dissertation is now available in the publication: PAYTON, S. (1984) *Developing Awareness of Print*, Off-set Publication No. 2, Educational Review, Faculty of Education, University of Birmingham.

Predisposing Factors in Early Literacy: A Case Study

Margaret van Lierop

This study sets out to investigate the processes which led to the precocious reading ability of one child and considers the implications for the teaching of reading.

Sonia recognized all the lower case letters at 20 months and several words by 24 months; by 3 years, she was reading simple booklets which centred on her own special interests. By 5 years, she was a voracious reader of full length adventure stories and continued thereafter to read widely. This is by no means a unique achievement; many studies have looked at reading in pre-school children (Krippner, 1963; Durkin, 1966; Reger, 1966; Söderbergh, 1971; Clark, 1976; Forester, 1977; Payton, 1984). This case study, supported by the recent research literature, suggests that early literacy arises from a combination of interrelated predisposing factors. Each of these will be considered in turn with examples from journals on Sonia's development (1973–7).

1 The Nature of the Environment

Durkin (1966) in *Children Who Read Early* found that the children's success was related mainly to parental attitudes, in particular the role of the mother in interaction with the child and to the child's interest in becoming a reader; the children tended to be persistent, readily absorbed and serious; most significantly forty-four out of forty-six of them were read to at home. Clark (1976) in *Young Fluent Readers*, a study of children who were already reading on entry to school at 5 years of age, found mothers' attitudes to be instrumental in facilitating the children's early reading; these mothers too were closely involved with their children, found them stimulating companions and enjoyed verbal interaction with them. The homes provided a general richness of experience, one aspect of which was a love of books; the children were introduced to books and read to at an early age. Forester (1977), in case studies of children who learned to read without direct teaching, attributed the children's abilities to stimulating homes where adults readily answered questions about reading and provided wide-ranging experiences with print. Reger (1966) in *The Child Who Could Read Before He Could Talk* also illustrated the role of the environment in beginning reading. Södergergh (1971), in a study of her own child concluded that literacy might be attained easily and naturally in an appropriate setting at the right time. Krippner's study (1963) *The Boy Who Read at 18 Months* revealed that although the child had a superior visual memory and general intelligence, he also had an extensive background of cultural experiences: books were always available, his parents were avid readers and willingly answered his questions about letters and words. Bissex (1980) whose son taught himself to write and to read, describes the environment in which the child grew up: he lived in a house full of print where he often saw his parents reading and writing. He had been read to nightly since the middle of his second year and had a collection of his own books as well as sets of letters and access to a typewriter. The progress towards literacy of Payton's daughter Cecilia was facilitated firstly by her responsiveness to environmental print and the world of stories and secondly to the fact that sympathetic adults were willing to answer her questions and to provide confirmation of her hypotheses about the printed word (Payton, 1984).

In all these studies, it seems clear that certain characteristics of the child interacted with those of the environment to promote early reading. Sonia's background had much in common with these early readers: she grew up in a symbol rich environment where reading, writing, drawing, painting and sculpting were daily activities, so the idea of representation was familiar to her. She was well aware that symbols of many kinds carried meaning: she observed her father at work in his studio, was fascinated by the transformation of lumps of clay into portraits, masks and abstract shapes and she knew whom the portrait busts and drawings in the studio represented. She not only handled clay in a purposeful way as she modelled her own 'sculptures', but had access to a wide range of art materials once she had learnt not to try and eat them. Van Allen (1976) considered understanding and responding to non-alphabetic symbol systems to be as important as reading the written word and that the reading of print is accelerated by experience of communicating in many other ways.

Sonia had an unusual capacity to become completely absorbed in her activities from a very early age and became very upset if interrupted. She had a close relationship with both parents, which included a high degree of verbal interaction. She was a responsive, imaginative and interesting baby and this encouraged further interaction resulting in very early comprehension of spoken language and pleasure in words, rhymes and verbal games. Her intense visual curiosity led to excitement over patterns, pictures, letters and writing and to her being shown picture books and later story books. Throughout her second year, mostly at her own request, she was read to for about two hours a day, so her early life was permeated with print.

Some of the circumstances which led to her early literacy were fortuitous: firstly, because she was mentally hyperactive and needed very little sleep, she crammed more stimulus and learning into each day than would a more placid baby. Secondly, she suffered from severe teething symptoms: it was possible to take her mind off discomfort by talking to her and later by reading to her; on 'bad days' she was read to for several hours, as stories were the only stimulus strong enough to divert her attention from her swollen gums. There are analogies here with Cushla, the severely handicapped child for whom books were a source of comfort and who also became highly literate, despite many problems (Butler, 1979). The third factor was the birth of Sonia's brother when she was 18 months old: the baby was breast-fed on demand and to avoid jealousy, Sonia was allowed to fetch some books and climb on the other knee with them. Thus the baby's feed times became additional story times for Sonia. As the infant turned out to be exceptionally hungry, Sonia's story sessions were frequent and prolonged. (This early exposure to books may have been a factor in the baby's early reading!) Also, following the baby's birth, Sonia became strongly attached to and identified with her father, whom she often observed engaged in literary or artistic activities. Finally, like the children studied by Durkin and Clark, Sonia had the advantage of having no artificial time scale for learning and was unhampered by pressure to progress. As she became ready, she was presented with suitable, meaningful reading material.

2 Cognitive Clarity: Functional and Featural Concepts of Literacy

Downing (1979) employs the term 'cognitive clarity' as the critical factor in developing reading skills; this involves a clear understanding of both functional and featural concepts of literacy.

(a) Functional Concepts of Literacy

Downing, Ollila and Oliver (1977) found that experiences in the home were important for developing an understanding of the communication process and the functions of reading and writing. The Bullock Report (DES, 1975) recommended that from the earliest stages of learning to read, emphasis should be placed on 'purpose, meaning and pleasure' and that children should learn how enjoyable and useful reading can be even before they can read for themselves: 'It is important that before the child begins to read for himself he must come to look upon reading as an activity with a purpose'. In a similar vein, Reid (1982) asserted that 'Before the actual learning of the code begins, the child must see something of the nature and aims of the task'.

Sonia grew up expecting written symbols to carry meaning: by the end of her second year, she was aware of the following functions of literacy: the enjoyment and creation of stories and the recording of information and messages. She understood that books meant stories and that it was the print as well as the picture which produced meaning: even before she could talk, she would point at the print as she engaged in pretend reading. She knew that messages were put in the milk bottle to tell the milkman how many bottles to leave and that we left a note to tell Daddy that we were going out. She also knew that letters landing on the doormat conveyed messages, often from people she knew. She recognized any airmail envelope as 'letter from Grandma'. Once, at 30 months Sonia replied to 'This looks like a letter from Grandma' with 'Oh good! Maybe she's coming home. Tell Sonia what it says!' She received invitations to birthday parties and took great interest in the writing of invitations for her second birthday party, in posting them herself through her friends' letter boxes and in the replies which arrived a few days later. In her third year, part of her bed-time ritual was asking her father to draw pictures for her; often she would tell him what to write beneath the picture and then seek out her mother to have the script read back, thereby confirming her developing notions about the nature of print. This supports the view of Hall (1976) that as children see their spoken thoughts put into written form, they can understand the nature of reading. The child thus learns to associate spoken with written words.

Smith (1978) stresses that children need to acquire the insight that differences in print are meaningful. At 23 months, Sonia was aware that print carried a message but had not made the conceptual leap that a word was always composed of the same letters. She once announced:

> 'Mummy, come see. Sonia make Mummy's name.'

She had selected the 'm' of her plastic letters and followed it by several more random letters. She was testing a hypothesis regarding spelling and evaluating feedback. Once she claimed to have made 'Daddy's name' but on being asked if she had made it with 'D' for Daddy and 'a' for apple, she crossly retorted:

> Not with 'a' for apple, silly Daddy, with *numbers*. Look!

Nevertheless, she always recognized the word 'Daddy' written down, but had not understood that there was only one way to write it. Similarly, she recognized the word 'Mummy' but once demanded that 'Mummy's name be written with "S" for Sonia in it'.

(b) Featural Concepts of Literacy

Francis (1982) found that success in reading was likely to devolve from an understanding of the concepts of letters, words and sentences and of the idea that the spoken word can be represented in print. Children who were late in acquiring these concepts were unable to appreciate many of the teachers' references to various aspects of reading. Clay (1975) pointed out that some children, even after months of instruction are uncertain about featural concepts. Reid (1982) also asserted that early understanding of concepts of print was an important factor in acquiring literacy skills.

Sonia started to develop an awareness of the concepts of print through a Ladybird alphabet book. She was shown it as a picture book but by 18 months, she was fascinated by the visual form of the lower case letters opposite each picture; she pointed them out with a querying 'Aa? Aa?' so was told the phonic names of the letters as she seemed to find these as interesting as the pictures. She loved to have an adult go through the book repeating: 'Here's "a" for apple and here's the apple' etc. She never tired of this and sometimes requested it many times a day. In this way, she was beginning to learn the general orthographic principle that letters represent sounds. Around this time, she was introduced to 'S' for Sonia and 'M' for Mummy. If she advanced on an adult carrying a pencil, she meant 'Write "S" for Sonia.' She would then point to her mother shouting 'Aa! Aa!' and point back to the bearer of the pencil meaning 'Write "M" for Mummy.' She studied the results carefully. Soon she started seeing 'S' for Sonia in newspaper headlines, street signs or on notices, which she would point out with 'Aa! Aa!' and point back to herself asking someone to verbalize what she had in mind. Awareness of print in the environment was a major factor in learning to read for the self-taught black child in Torrey's study (1973). Bissex (1980) attributed her child's success in writing and reading to the fact that he grew up in a print-filled world.

The letter concept Sonia was forming was aided by a set of plastic letters inset into a board. By 20 months, the letters were more than symbols; they were objects in their own right and could be investigated visually, manually and orally. She was able to assimilate such abstract concepts as letters into her cognitive framework by personalizing them, thereby relating them to what she knew already. Similarly, in her imaginative play, any inanimate object might be endowed with a personality and feelings. The plastic letters were welcomed into a rich world of imagination, each assuming its own identity (see appendix A); particularly interesting was the letter 'q', known to her as 'q' for Quilty (ie an old pram quilt, her constant companion and source of comfort). In Quilty's absence, the 'q' assumed Quilty's identity, as she held it to her cheek, murmuring 'Quilty' in her most loving voice or made it kiss her when she hurt herself. The detachable numbers of Sonia's clock also became personalities, alternately in conflict and friendly; she devised treats and punishments for various numbers, always addressing them correctly by name: 'Poor number 7 is tired 'cos he's always standing on one leg.' Söderbergh's 2 year-old daughter is reported as treating words denoting persons or things as if they were those persons or things and flashcards bearing emotionally significant words (for example, grandmother and grandfather) immediately became favourites.

It appears that the concept of a word is particularly difficult for young children. Donaldson (1978) points out that many children have problems learning to read because they do not realize that the flow of speech can be broken into separate words, adding that, 'this realization is indispensable if they are to deal sensibly with the grouped and spaced marks on paper, which as they must now come to see, correspond with the spoken language'. De Villiers (1979) comments on the difficulty of segmenting speech when one does not know about the units as there are no pauses between words. Luria (1946), cited by Elkonin (1971) refers to the analogy of glass: as a child looks through glass at the world, so it looks through a word to the meaning, the word itself not being an object of awareness. In the early stages of learning to read, according to Luria, 'a word, as a unit of the system of language, for the first time acquires its own concreteness and sensitivity, it becomes an object of child's awareness.'

Sonia's word concept began to evolve around 20 months when she was admiring some writing: the word 'Sonia' was pointed out to her. She was so fascinated that it was written on a piece of card. She studied it closely, pointing to the individual letters. Flashcards were made of Sonia, Ben, Mummy, Daddy, Quilty and Rabbit (a favourite toy with a strong personality). Thereafter she frequently played with them and compared them, placing 'names' on people or helping Rabbit to put the wrong 'names' on people, an activity which caused her much mirth. She particularly liked the dots on the 'i's and 'j's and indicated with pleasure that her name, Quilty's and Rabbit's all had dots, whereas Mummy, Daddy and Ben did not have dots. Gradually she acquired more flashcards all of which were incorporated into her world of play and imagination: she had to go into the garden to show the trees their 'name' while 'telephone's name' had to stay on the telephone all day 'So telephone remember it.' She was frequently seen studying print in books: once, at 2.7, she was found kissing the print in a Ladybird reading book and explained: 'Sonia's kissing this little "a" all by itself.' All the other letters were in groups, but little 'a' was often seen alone thus inspiring the affectionate and protective feelings she felt for anything small. Her word concept was reinforced by the rediscovery of her Ladybird alphabet book. She talked to herself as she perused it: 'Look! There's "a" for apple and there's apple's name. There's "e" for elephant and there's elephant's long name,' etc (2.3). While she was aware that sentences were made up of 'names', she could not appreciate the concept of word order or direction. At 2.5, she said: 'Look

Mummy! Sonia's made "I like Daddy"' She had arranged the cards into "Daddy like I".

3 Reading Aloud to Children: The Implications for Learning to Read.

Reading aloud to children has been stressed perhaps above all else in recent years as an important predisposing factor in the acquisition of literacy.' Every time a parent reads aloud to a child, the child is learning that by some curious means the lines of print can be converted into stories which he can enjoy.' (The Bullock Report, DES 1975). Smith (1978): 'Children learn to read with the first intuition that print is meaningful or the first time they hear a story read aloud.' The benefits to the would-be reader tend to be classified under:

(a) the enjoyment of reading and the fostering of positive attitudes;
(b) gaining insights into the purpose of literacy and concepts of print;
(c) the development of linguistic awareness conducive to the acquisition of reading skills.

The first of these is emphasized by Carol Chomsky (1972), who speculates that a child whose mother reads to him 'learns to assign a special role to reading, for what his mother enjoys doing with him, he naturally comes to enjoy and recognize as a valued activity.' This was certainly true of the *Young Fluent Readers* described by Clark (Clark, 1976), as their parents enjoyed their books with them. Goodman and Altwerger (1981) in their study of literacy development also recommended reading aloud to children and providing them with first hand experience of books. Weaver (1980) too stresses this aspect: 'It is particularly important to read to children at first just in order for them to learn the purpose of books and the joys of reading'.

Sonia's enjoyment of books was undoubtedly a factor in her early reading; she was insatiable in her demand for stories often requesting the same one many times. By the time Sonia was 3 and her brother 18 months, her mother's journals frequently complained of the amount of time spent reading stories: 'Every time I come to the end of a book, Sonia pleads for more and Ben screws up his face threatening to cry.' The idea of pleasure from books was familiar very early: at 2.11, Sonia asked: 'Mummy, how lonely were you when you didn't have your little children? Did you read lots of books?'

Clark (1976) considered that reading to children 'is part of the process of learning the characteristics of written language and, therefore, an integral part of the reading instruction'. The language of the stories read to Sonia was carefully graded according to her level of comprehension, progressing from the labelling of pictures at 8 months to CS Lewis *Narnia* stories at 5 years. When she came to independent reading, she was already familiar with the formal features of book language and the more complex linguistic structures of stories. In a sense, she grew up 'bilingual', learning the language of books simultaneously with colloquial speech, so she did not have to make the adjustment of many 5 year olds learning to read.

A child who is read to has more opportunities to absorb the rules of grammatical structure: Clay (1979) found that children with high skills in handling inflections could use this in error correction behaviour. Merritt (1969) postulated that intermediate skills (fluency) depend on the ability to respond to different kinds of sequence: a knowledge of the syntactic features of language limits the range of choices and reduces uncertainty. By 3 years, Sonia had mastered the basic grammar of standard English and syntactically knew what to expect in stories. Clark (1976) observed that, 'The more a child has become sensitized to the structure of written language, the more he is likely to make appropriate anticipations when reading for himself.' She hypothesized that frequent repetition of stories may lead to improved ability to predict one's way through print, by anticipating the correct word or words. This was confirmed in Sonia's case: at 15 months, before she could talk, she was making predictions: if in a story, she noticed an omission from a previous reading, she would point questioningly and persistently at the appropriate part of the picture until the missing detail was supplied. At 17 months, when her father was reading to her, he absent-mindedly said: 'This little pussy cat said "Woof"' She jerked herself upright, pointed amusedly at the cat and said 'Woof?' and started to laugh, relishing the incongruity and refusing to let him correct himself.

Sonia's thorough knowledge of story language became a useful tool when she started to read independently as she was able to make appropriate anticipations. Some of her early reading was from stories which she had often heard read aloud, (*The Gingerbread Boy*, *The Enormous Turnip* etc): although many of the words were still difficult, her fluency was aided by the familiarity and predictability of the text, which she partly read, partly remembered and partly guessed. Thus she had sufficient non-visual cues to 'pick up' what she could not decode. In Smith's terms, she was 'learning to read by reading', confirming his notion that reading is 'a matter of increasing returns.'

4 Suitable Early Reading Material

Subject matter which is personally significant is most likely to lead to success in early reading. This is the essence of the language experience approach which according to Downing (1979) 'consists in using the child's own language and experiences to construct his personal materials for reading.' Goddard (1974) claimed that early experience with reading and writing should be linked with the child's own preoccupations, giving expression to his own thoughts, feelings and experiences.

Sonia was helped to conceptualize reading as speech written down through the making of books about highly emotive aspects of her environment: exciting experiences and important characters, particularly 'Rabbit' and 'Quilty'. If an event captured her imagination, she wanted it recounted many times and would act it out. At 22 months, she frequently asked: 'Daddy, tell Sonia 'bout Rabbit getting lost in Birmingham'; she also re-enacted the scene many times pretending to be Daddy running back to retrieve Rabbit. Finally a book was made about the incident (appendix B), the first of many 'Adventures of Rabbit'. Using the pictures as cues, she happily 'read' the story both to herself and to Rabbit. Story telling became a favourite occupation and everyday in the bath she entertained her brother with elaborate accounts of the 'other life' of Rabbit and Quilty, all narrated in her best story telling voice. By her fourth year, she was dictating her own 'Rabbit' books and asking her father to illustrate them (appendix C). When her own story was read back to her and clearly illustrated, she needed no explanations of the meaning and function of print. This further confirms Hall's claim that 'As children see their spoken thoughts put into written form, they can understand the nature of communication in reading in addition to recognizing words.' As soon as Sonia could write, she made books for herself, her little brother and her toys; by 5 years, she was writing and illustrating long, untidy and highly imaginative stories in booklets which she then tried to sell to her friends (appendix D).

Ashton-Warner (1963) felt strongly that a child's first reading words must have intense meaning and be part of the child's own being. Early reading material is welcomed eagerly when it reflects the child's own world. Sonia's first reading book did this: its heroes were Quilty, Little Flower and Big Flower (important decorations on Quilty), Rabbit, Mummy, Daddy and Ben. Semantically and syntactically, it was simple, but most important, it had strong emotional appeal. The success of this booklet led to the making of many subsequent ones, all reflecting her current interests and increasing skills in tackling print. Nevertheless there was a wide discrepancy between the little reading booklets and the kind of stories she most enjoyed. The gap was bridged by finding a graded reading scheme which appealed to her. She showed no interest in the older traditional schemes but was delighted by the mundane characters of Peter and Jane of the Ladybird scheme. Before reading each page, she perused the minutest detail of the illustrations commenting on what Peter and Jane might do next. Initially some non-content words posed problems. 'Here is a tree' did not reflect the speech she heard or used, nor was it part of story language. Sonia tended to read 'Jane has a dog' as 'Jane got a dog' and if corrected, said it was 'a silly book'. After a few weeks, she had acquired enough 'reading book language' to continue working through the scheme.

After several Ladybird reading books, she found she could read other books, in particular a series about Andy Pandy and Teddy (her favourite characters in fiction at the time). From this stage, her reading accelerated rapidly: the more she read, the more she found she could read. By 4.10 she had read all the Ladybird books up to 12b and had read for herself the stories which had been read to her over the previous three years.

Thus it appears, that if reading material has high personal interest, the child naturally becomes a reader for meaning. Smith (1978) maintained that the fluent reader constucts the meaning by eliminating unlikely alternatives. This process is facilitated if the syntax and content of the material conform to the child's expectations. If the material is derived from the child's own frame of reference, the problems of bringing meaning to print are minimized.

Conclusion: Implications for the Teaching of Reading

What emerges from a study of Sonia's early literacy is that it was not grafted artificially on to her experience, but was woven into the entire fabric of her early life. Story books were a source of stimulus, pleasure and comfort and she moved happily from listening to stories and looking at picture books to independent reading, as naturally as she learned to talk. This corroborates Smith's theory that while reading cannot be formally taught, if the scene is correctly set, the child will learn spontaneously; the teacher then becomes the facilitator and guide who modifies circumstances, responds to the child's needs and makes reading meaningful. In Weaver's words (1980) 'we cannot really "teach them to read" any more than we can teach them to talk. But we *can* provide appropriate stimulation and guidance'. McInnes (1973) also makes the point that reading should not be an isolated subject in the curriculum, unrelated to the development of thought and language. He warns that teachers should not dissociate the reading act from the rest of the child's growth and use procedures that have little relevance for the child.

It could be postulated that any normal child, given favourable conditions, would grow naturally into enjoying reading, obviating the need to isolate it as a serious school subject, always referred to as *work* rather than play or recreation and often associated with pressure, tension and potential failure.

Children who read early tend to come from stimulating and emotionally warm homes where they have experienced positive relationships with adults, who through sensitive and unobtrusive observation have provided them with opportunities for learning at the right time. It might be argued that *all children* should be introduced to literacy in a warm, secure and accepting environment. The fostering of positive attitudes towards literacy is, in the writer's experience, best achieved through *carefully selected stories*. All children, no matter how limited their experience of language or how 'deprived' their background, quickly learn to love stories, at first told in language close to their own and gradually elaborated as they develop a greater understanding of the complexities of discourse structure. Donaldson and Reid (1982) recommend reading aloud as it helps to familiarize children with new more complex linguistic forms, while the living voice helps to bring out the meaning, with amplification and explanation if needed. If story telling and reading were central to nursery and infant curricula, rather than a gesture at the end of the school day, children would be exposed to a wider range of vocabulary and linguistic structure, they would be awakened to the functions of literacy and their powers of imagination and concentration would be enhanced. If teacher and children were enjoying together the world of print, learning would take place.

Children can be shown how salient experiences can be preserved and savoured by recording them in writing and drawing; if booklets are made for and with groups of children centred on their own activities, they are highly motivated to read them. If the wording is generated by the children, it will reflect their own language, be easily predictable and have high interest value. Modern reprographic techniques facilitate the production of booklets centred on the children's own experience. The teacher can capitalize on their pleasure in recounting experiences or telling stories by tape recording and transcribing their narrative before they can read or write, thereby assisting the development of functional and featural concepts of literacy. Indeed, *The Bullock Report* (DES, 1975) advocated a language experience approach along these lines.

Above all, the acquisition of literacy in schools, as in the homes of young fluent readers, must take place in a child-centred environment. The child needs an adult who can observe his frame of reference and adapt materials and methods to suit him. 'Informed teachers are capable of learning more about students from careful observation and interactions than they can from test scores' (Goodman and Altwerger, 1981). As with children who read early, children in infant schools can acquire concepts about print and literacy with little formal teaching. Teachers need to set the scene carefully and then have the confidence to allow the child to come to reading in his own time. As with the acquisition of spoken language, children need time to absorb before they can produce. If given wide and positive experience of print in an undemanding, anxiety-free situation, the child will eventually learn quickly, but more important he will learn to enjoy books.

Appendix A

By 20 months, most of the letters of Sonia's plastic alphabet set had become personified and had definite characters and associations, often linked to the pictures of the Ladybird ABC book.

On picking up the letter 'a' she would say 'apple', pretend to bite, offer some to her parents and pretend to pull out and throw away the stalk. For the 'b' she would shout 'balloon', blow and say 'pop'. For the 'c' she said 'cake', pretended to eat some and blew; (memories of birthday cake candles). For 'd' she said 'duck' and made it quack. She did not name 'e' possibly because she could not say the word 'elephant', (the appropriate picture in the ABC book). 'g' and 'h' had no particular character; she called them 'gate' and 'house' respectively. She always loved 'i' for ink, because of the dot on top and tended to call it 'dot, dot, dot'. By this time she had finally managed to distinguish it from 'j', which she called 'jug' and pretended to pour from. 'k' was a favourite and 'kekkle' did long sessions of pouring out imaginary tea for everyone to drink. 'l' for lion did very realistic growls. 'm' for Mummy was often one of the first to be singled out. 'n' for nail was very boisterous and 'bang-banged' all around the room. 'o' for orange was the all time favourite, mainly for aesthetic reasons; the shape had always fascinated her. 'p' for postman was a comparative nonentity. 'q' for Quilty was a favourite because it represented Quilty. 'r' for Rabbit was as mischievous as Rabbit himself; it would hop all round the room with Sonia shouting 'hop! hop! hop!' The 'r' like Rabbit, was also very rude and was often heard to indulge in unprovoked outbursts of spitting (sound effects by Sonia), while Sonia exuberantly shouted 'Rude! Rude!' 's' for Sonia was frequently commented upon and shown to anyone who happened to be around. 't' for table and 'u' for umbrella had no particular character. 'v' for van occasionally brum-brummed around the room. 'w' for window was not considered very exciting. The 'x' which she called 'criss-cross' was always treated very lovingly; she liked to carry it round, repeating 'criss-cross' in an affectionate little voice. 'y' for yellow was another nonentity, but the 'z' which she called 'zebra' often 'geed-up' quite excitedly.

Appendix B

Extract from a 'Rabbit' book made for Sonia at 1 year 10 months.

Daddy ran back to the
bus stop as fast as he
could Rabbit was naughty
all the way to the bus stop
He jumped along the wall
by the pavement and
made Sonia laugh
They nearly missed the bus.
10

On the bus, Rabbit was very naughty again. He wouldn't sit quietly on Sonia's knee He kept jumping on to the floor and Daddy had to pick him up, all the way to the station Daddy was very cross with Rabbit.

11

On the train, Rabbit was tired and he went to sleep Mummy and Daddy were very glad, because Rabbit had been a nuisance all day.

12.

When we got home, Mummy and Daddy said: "Rabbit's not coming to Birmingham again. Next time, we'll take some good toys.

13.

Appendix C

Extracts from a 'Rabbit' book dictated by Sonia — one of a series. 4 years 5 months.

.... he landed on a spaceman!

4.

The spaceman told him off

5.

Rabbit sat on the spaceman!

6.

Then Rabbit made friends with the spaceman and they went for a ride in a moon car.

7.

Appendix D

Extract from story written by Sonia at 5 years.

Once upon a time ther Was a little peg and it Was Wight and all the other pegs laughed at him. They were brown pegs. The lady Who Was hanging up the clothes. Saw the unusual peg and put it on the line.

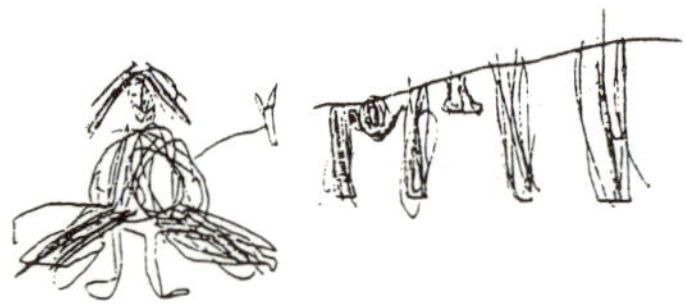

The peg on the line that Was Wight Was not happy he did not like it on the line. but he fell of the line and a bird got out of his nest and picked it up.

he flew to Africa. Then the peg Was not happy and he fell into the well and Was not seen again But a bird got out of his nist and flew into the well and he went and picked it up.

But What a shock the bird got. he could not find the Way out of the well He Was trapped in the well somebody had put a stone over the well shaft. two children were having a walk in the field and Saw the well and thought that the well Shaft Was fun and they were happy But the well moved and the children were frightened

References

ASHTON-WARNER, S. (1963) *Teacher*, London, Secker and Warburg.

BISSEX, G.L. (1980) *Gnys at Wrk: A Child Learns to Read and Write* Cambridge, Mass. Harvard University Press.

BUTLER, D. (1979) *Cushla and her Books*, London Hodder and Stoughton.

CHOMSKY, C. (1972) 'Stages in language development and reading exposure', *Harvard Educational Review*, 42, 1, February.

CLARK, M.M. (1976) *Young Fluent Readers*, London, Heinemann.

CLAY, M.M. (1972) *Reading: The Patterning of Complex Behaviour*, Auckland, Heinemann.

CLAY, M.M. (1975) *What Did I Write? Beginning Writing Behaviour*, London, Heinemann.

DEPARTMENT OF EDUCATION AND SCIENCE (1975) *A Language for Life*, (The Bullock Report), London, HMSO.

DONALDSON, M. (1978) *Children's Minds*, Fontana/Collins.

DONALDSON, M. and REID, J.F. (1982) 'Language skills and reading: A developmental perspective' in HENDRY A. (Ed.) *Teaching Reading The Key Issues*, London, Heinemann.

DOWNING, J.A. (1979) *Reading and Reasoning*, Edinburgh, Chambers.

DOWNING, J.A., OLLILA, L. and OLIVER, P. (1977) 'Concepts of language in children from differing socio-economic backgrounds', *Journal of Educational Research*, 70, pp. 277–81.

DURKIN, D. (1966) *Children Who Read Early*, New York, Teacher's College Press.

FORESTER, A.D. (1977) 'What teachers can learn from 'natural readers', *The Reading Teacher*, 31, 2, November, pp. 160–6.

FRANCIS, H. (1982) *Learning to Read: Literate Behaviour and Orthographic Knowledge*, London, Allen and Unwin.

GODDARD, N. (1974) *Literacy: Language-Experience Approaches*, London, MacMillan.

GOODMAN, Y.M. and ALTWERGER, B. (1981) *Print Awareness in Pre-school Children: A Working Paper. A Study of the Development of Literacy in Pre-school Children*, Programme in Language and Literacy, University of Arizona.

HALL, M. (1976) *Teaching Reading as a Language Experience*, Columbus, Ohio, Merrill.

KRIPPNER, S. (1963) 'The boy who read at eighteen months', *Exceptional Children*, 30, pp. 105–9.

LURIA, A.R. and ELKONIN D.B. (1971) Development of speech, in ZAPOROZHETS A.V. and ELKONIN D.B. (Eds) *The Psychology of Pre-school Children*, Cambridge, Mass, MIT Press.

MCINNES, J.A. (1973) 'Language pre-requisites for reading', in CLARK, M.M. and MILNE A. (Eds) *Reading and Related Skills*, London, Ward Lock Educational, pp. 100–4.

MERRITT, J. (1969) 'The intermediate skills' in GARDNER K. (Ed.) *Reading Skills: Theory and Practice*, London, Ward Lock Educational.

PAYTON, S. (1984) *Developing Awareness of Print: A Young Child's First Steps Towards Literacy*, Educational Review, Off-set Publication No. 2, University of Birmingham.

REGER, R. (1966) 'The child who could read before he could talk', *Journal of School Psychology*, 4, 2, pp. 50–5.

REID, J. (1983) 'Into print: Reading and language growth', in DONALDSON, M. GRIEVE, R. and PRATT, C. (Eds) *Early Childhood Development and Education: Readings in Psychology*, Oxford, Blackwell.

SMITH, F. (1978) *Understanding Reading*, (2nd edn.) New York, Holt, Rinehart and Winston.

SÖDERBERGH, R. (1971) *Reading in Early Childhood*, Stockholm, Almqvist and Wiksell.
TORREY, J.W. (1973) 'Learning to read without a teacher', in SMITH, F. (Ed.) *Psycholinguistics and Reading*, New York, Holt, Rinehart and Winston.
VAN ALLEN, R. (1976) *Language Experiences in Communication*, Boston, Houghton Mifflin Co.
DE VILLIERS, P.A. and J.G. (1979) *Early Language*, Fontana.
WEAVER, C. *Psycholinguistics and Reading: From Process to Practice*, Cambridge, Mass, Winthrop.

Part 3. Reading and Writing: Reciprocal Relationships

Introduction

The first paper in this section is by Ferreiro, a developmental psychologist who worked originally in Argentina, then with Piaget in Geneva, and is now based in Mexico City. Her theme in this paper, which is developed in more extended form elsewhere, is that young children have begun to interpret the written system in consistent ways before they can read and write and that it is important to take account of these interpretations in planning initial literacy instruction. Ferreiro's empirical studies of young children's early interpretations of print have included children in different countries, and from illiterate homes as well as those from homes where literacy is an important and valued aspect of everyday life. In this paper the focus is insights from longitudinal studies of pre-school children and their efforts in the search for an understanding of 'the laws of the system' (of alphabetic writing). She indicates the importance of appreciating the children's developing awareness of print and also the fact that, like scientists, they will cling to their hypotheses not as yet ready to drop them at the first obstacle in their application. This shows the importance of providing young children with a variety of experiences selected to assist them in extending or modifying their hypotheses as needed for a full understanding of the featural and functional aspects of print.

The second paper, by Frith a cognitive psychologist, shows the insights to be gained by a cognitive approach to understanding the relationship of spelling and reading and explores them in the context of spelling reform. The need for spelling reformers to consider reading (input) and writing (output) processes separately in their own right is noted. Frith stresses the extent to which the reader tends to rely on a variety of cues present in conventional English orthography which may relate to meaning, origin and syntactic function.

The final paper in this section, by Barr, written for this publication, develops further the theme introduced by Frith. With illustrations from two recent major research projects based in secondary schools, one on reading and the other on writing, Barr indicates their parallel concerns in seeking to analyze the features necessary for purposeful reflective reading and writing. The importance of analyzing the features specific to reading and to writing is stressed and also the extent to which aspects such as cohesion in text are important for both. The theme of cohesion is one which will be explored in the following section. There are implications from the paper by Barr and from those in the following section, for instruction in, and a curriculum for, the language arts in secondary education and in upper primary (elementary) school. In earlier sections the importance of cognition in understanding the task of reading was emphasized: here the importance of each of the language arts of reading and writing as 'powerful tools in the development of reflective thinking' (and cognition) is stressed.

The Relationship between Oral and Written Language: The Children's Viewpoints★

Emilia Ferreiro

The relationship between oral and written language seems obvious to any literate adult. What else could the letters represent except the elementary sounds of the speech, even though this representation could only be approximate? What else could the series of letters with blanks in between represent except the words that we pronounce when we speak?

It is difficult for us to imagine that someone may not look at writing in this way. We do know that there are individuals who cannot interpret writing as we do (illiterate adults and preschool children). However this 'cannot interpret writing as we do' is looked at as a 'they cannot' or as a 'they do not know.'

The objective of this paper is to show how, long before knowing how to read and write in the conventional meaning of these terms, children are able to interpret in a consistent way — but in a way that is entirely different from ours — the written system that is our own. Moreover, our aim will be to show: (1) that there are modes of interpretations genetically ordered, preceding the acceptance of the basic hypothesis concerning the alphabetic system; (2) that such modes of interpretations, coming earlier in the development, are constituent parts of the final modes of interpretations (i.e. of those modes that are in agreement with the structure of the alphabetic system; (3) that writing — inasmuch as it is a socially established cultural object — is an object of knowledge, and that, being so, it imposes requirements to logical thinking, as much as it depends on the possibilities of assimilation which are determined by the logical structure of the subject.

We have studied this evolution through a multiple approach technique by applying the method of critical exploration which is characteristic

★ Originally published in GOODMAN, Y.M. *et al.* (Eds) (1980) *Oral and Written Language Development Research: Impact on the Schools*, National Council of Teachers of English.

of Piagetian studies. The general hypotheses that we put forward received their first validation through the data we obtained in our first series of studies carried out in Buenos Aires (Ferreiro and Teberosky, 1979). Afterwards, research conducted in Geneva and in Monterrey (Mexico) (Ferreiro *et al.*, 1979) allowed us to go into more depth concerning some essential aspects of the problem. More recently, we were able to add a new dimension to our work through research carried out in Mexico City: a longitudinal study of a group of thirty children between three and six years of age whom we followed during a period of two years. They were selected in accordance with one variable which is fundamental for our work: Children of illiterate or semi-illiterate parents living under conditions of extreme poverty, on the one hand; and children of parents with university education who, because of their profession and/or way of living, make daily use of the written language, on the other. The examples that I will use to support the theses I present will come from this last kind of investigation.

From the multiple aspects of the evolution that we have studied I have selected one in particular: the evolution of the 'spontaneous' writing (that is, the writing that is not the product of a particular training, nor the immediate reproduction of an external model).

Let us accept that those children, when they write, make an approximate correspondence between sounds and letters. They may face orthography problems, but they do not have any further problems with writing, because they are now functioning inside the alphabetical system of writing. In order to understand how they have reached that point, it is necessary to understand the conceptions of, for example, those children who have started writing with actual letters, but do not require that two words beginning with the same sound should also begin with the same letter. We also need to understand the conceptions that are at work even before that, as in the case of those children who write with unconventional signs, but organize the elements of their production in a linear order, very different from the order of the elements composing a drawing.

We will take as a starting point — for the purpose of this paper — the precise moment when we find a differentiation between two kinds of graphic representations: the drawing and the writing. When they start behaving as scriptors, children note the difference between what they conceptualize as a drawing (which they call by a name following the indefinite article) and what they think to be a piece of writing (waving line, or series of straight or circular strokes).

Silvia (a little girl of the slums) undergoes, in eleven months, the following evolution: series of circles without linearity (4.1), series of circles with linearity (4.8), a single circle for each name of an object of which the representation is intended (5.0).

A single grapheme for each image of an object is also a decisive moment in the evolution of Fernando (4.11), of Delfino (3.9), of Jorge (3.3), and of Nanis (3.10), all slum children.

The next step is a very important one: the requirement of various graphemes for the writing of a single name. At the moment this requirement starts being exhibited, the amount of letter-like forms being utilized is quite variable, and the variations do not correspond to any criterion which may be considered as objective: The child knows that he needs several letters, without knowing how many, and without knowing any reason that may determine the range of variability of such an amount.

A short time after, however, such a 'fluid' quantity is replaced by an internal organizing mechanism: a minimum quantity — which sometimes has a tendency to become a fixed quantity — below which one cannot go without going against the 'readability' (that is, the intelligibility) of the text.

This requirement of a minimum quantity demands some comments because it has a decisive influence in the following evolution. From the beginning of our research, in 1975, we used a classification task with the following instruction: Which cards are good for reading? (i.e., which ones are 'readable.') The cards showed single letters or numbers; strings of two, three, four, five, and six letters (displaying either real words or impossible combinations like XYZ); real or pseudo-letters (in isolation or in combination); strings of four letters all the same; capitals and hand written; etc. We did not ask children to read the cards, but only to determine whether the cards showed what is necessary for a reading act. Ambiguous as it is, this instruction nevertheless elicited a striking behavioral consistency among children, and allowed us to establish that a minimum number of characters and their variety are the most important characteristics of a 'readable' string. (The same criterion was found by Lavine (1977) using a different instruction, as she asked for criteria for writing and not for readability.) A card with the same letter repeated is rejected, because 'It is always the same one; it cannot be read,' and a card with one or two graphemes — even if they are real letters — is also rejected, because 'There must be several ones.' Even if children often find it difficult to make explicit the 'how many' of the 'several ones,' their classification shows that the critical number is three (actually the minimum number of characters demanded for readability is 3 ± 1).

This same 'magic' number three is also demanded in their own production of a piece of writing (very often this requirement of a minimum quantity appears in spontaneous writing before it is shown as a classfication criterion; that is, it is shown before in contexts where the writing is interpreted th n in contexts where only the formal characteristics of the writing are exhibited, outside any interpretative context).

Starting with this internal control of the minimum quantity, a series of new possibilities will emerge.

(A) The quantity of letters may increase as a function of quantitative variations of the referent (they use more letters for a big house than for a small house).

(B) At the beginning the intention of the scriptor is of primary importance for the interpretation: Identical texts or very similar ones may serve to represent names of very different objects, as much as very different texts may serve to represent identical names. Gradually two complementary requirements begin to establish: In order to read different things there must exist an objective difference in the writing; and in order to read similar things there must exist an objective similarity (although not identity) in the writing. In other words, the conceptual identity must be reflected in the representation, as much as the conceptual difference. (The primacy of conceptual similarity over sound similarity becomes evident when, for instance, children write with similar letters 'gallina' (hen) and 'pollitos' (little chickens).)

(C) These intentional variations in the produced representations are limited by three fundamental factors: the requirement of minimum quantity, the requirement of internal variety (to avoid repeating twice — or more than twice — the same letter), and the stock of letters that is at the disposal of the child.

Under the strong constraints of these internal requirements (quantity and variety) and also being limited by their own stock of letters at their disposal, some children make a great exploit: the discovery that variations in the linear order of the same elements produce different totalities. This is nothing less than the beginning of the understanding of the permutations and combinations, in the midst of the pre-operatory period and much before the letters acquire a relationship to sound.

Until here, the writing is interpreted in a global way, in the following sense: to the whole constituted by the series of letters corresponds another whole that is the stated name. However, this whole (totality) has its parts and children's preference for writing with separate characters (printing-form letters) seems to be justified by the need to be sure of the required minimum quantity. The relationship between the totality and the parts becomes understandable when the quantity of objects is taken as a criterion for the determination of the quantity of letters (six letters for a set of six apples, for instance); nevertheless, what could be the value of each letter when the referent is unique? In attempting to solve this problem, children make a decisive step: To one part of the writing they match one part of the name. The partition of the written name is given by each individual letter. The partition of the name at the oral level is not given: It must be found out. In the search for those parts of the name the child arrives at the syllabic decomposition (Bellefroid and Ferreiro, 1979). Here the syllabic hypothesis emerges for the first time: To each written letter corresponds one syllable of the name that was intended to be written. For the first time there is a clear relationship between the writing and the formal aspects of the speech. This relationship is not yet the conventional relation; it is rather a hypothesis that points in the correct direction, insofar as it links the written representation with formal aspects of the speech.

The syllabic hypothesis suffers multiple ups and downs. It is not constituted straight off, and it has to compete with alternative hypotheses (such as the correspondence with other quantitative aspects of the referent). Initially, it is far from being strict: like the genesis of other term-to-term correspondences (for example, the number) it starts admitting omissions and repetitions before requiring that each term of one of the series should correspond to one, and only one, of the other series. Thus, at the beginning of this period children can read syllabically, but jump letters or repeat syllables as is needed to reach the end. Because before serving to foresee the construction, to determine in advance the quantity of letters, the syllabic hypothesis serves to justify the writing already made. This syllabic reading adjusts itself initially to the text already produced and considered as a finished product. The written letters are there; they cannot be erased. The child needs to adjust the reading to what is already produced, as if it were produced by someone else.

It is only much later, at the peak of syllabic hypothesis, that two new behaviors are exhibited: the possibility of erasing letters if it is found that there are too many when the child proceeds to verifying reading, and the possibility of utilizing the syllabic hypothesis to anticipate the necessary amount of letters before writing them.

During the period when the syllabic hypothesis is in force, the requirement of minimum amount remains. The coexistence of both requirements (one letter for each syllable and a total not less than two or three letters) is at the source of new conflicts, this time with reference to the writing of monosyllabic words (and sometimes — depending on the minimum amount — also with the bisyllabic words). In fact, in accordance with the syllabic hypothesis, a monosyllabic word should be written with only one letter; however, in accordance with the requirement of minimum amount, only one letter is not enough.

We shall take as an example the evolution during one calendar year of two children, one from the middle class (Mariana) and another from a slum (Javier), who have the advantage of presenting an evolution which is relatively slow, in spite of the fact that both children are clever and rather precocious in their operatory development. (Javier achieves conservation of number at 5.2 and Mariana did the same at 4.6.)

Javier:

4.7 — He utilizes a repertoire which is limited to eight graphemes, where he mixes forms corresponding to letters with forms corresponding to numbers. For each new piece of writing he is careful in changing the order of the graphemes and in maintaining the internal variability. Example:

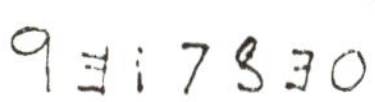 'mandarinas' (tangerines)

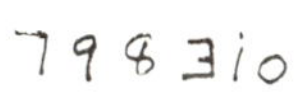 'chícharos' (peas)

The amount of graphemes varies between three and nine, and there is no indication of any objective criterion to regulate it.

4.10 — The amount of graphemes increases if the amount of objects increases, and the conceptual similarity is reflected in the writing. Example:

ΛPiO	'gato' (cat: one cat in the picture)
rpioriPo	'gatitos' (little cats: three cats in the picture)

5.0 — The foregoing characteristics are maintained.

5.5 — He utilizes a minimum of three letters; the amount of letters may increase in accordance with the quantitative variations of the referent. Example:

OtP	'mosca' (fly)
PnPoP	'vaca' (cow)
Aoi	'gato' (cat)
OiA	'gatito' (little cat)
OAiOAiOAi	'gatitos' (three little cats in the picture; he explains as he is writing: 'one little cat' (the first three letters), 'the little cats here' (six letters), 'another cat' (the three remaining letters).

There is, however, at the same time an attempt of syllabic analysis: when one tries to get him back to his own writing he makes a syllabic reading:

OAi	A oi
'ga-ti-ta'	'ga-to'
(little cat)	(cat)

5.7 — He starts utilizing the syllabic hypothesis in order to foresee the number of letters.

5.10 — Systematic utilization of the syllabic hypothesis in order to forecast the amount of letters. He anticipates that "vaca" will take two letters, the first one being 'la va.' He first puts two dots, to indicate two places, and then he puts letters on them. The syllabic anticipation is rigorous in all words having at least two syllables:

Λo	'vaca' (cow)
OiOE	'mariposa' (butterfly)
OFEΛ	'elefante' (elephant)

However, for the monosyllabic words he writes also two letters, giving up the syllabic analysis. In order to appreciate the difference, one may compare:

How many do you need to write 'mariposa'?	'ma-ri-po-sa' —— four!
How many do you need to write 'pan'? (bread)	'pan? pann? —— two!'  'pan'

It should be observed that all this evolution is prior to the attribution of a stable sound-value — whether or not it be conventional — to the letters. We should also take into consideration that Javier, in spite of being the child of illiterate parents, has some school-type information through his elder brothers, that he knows at 5 years the names of letters and numbers, and that at 5½ he knows the initial of his name, the vowels, and the numbers to ten.

Mariana: (She is the daughter of university professors; she also has a sister who is several years older)

3.6 — One letter is enough to write the name of an animal as big as an elephant. However criteria for quantity appear already outlined in some situations.

3.9 — The syllabic analysis of words starts as a guideline for the quantity of letters, but she searches for a space coincident with the length of the image, and this spatial consideration takes over the syllabic control. Example:

 She writes 'taza' (cup) saying at the same time 'ta-za'.

She sees that something is left in order to cover the length of the image and makes the following comment: "No, there is much left out." She adds letters until she reaches the space frontier, at both sides of the initial writing:

Afterwards, she attempts without success to read what she wrote: 'ta-za'; 'taaaza'; 'taaazaaa'; etc., without being satisfied.

4.0 — She attempts combinations over a limited repertoire of four letters:

 (The picture shows a cock over a fence. First line, 'gallo' (cock); second line 'palos' (horizontal sticks); third line 'palos' (vertical sticks).)

When she reads she adjusts her interpretation to the hypothesis of two letters for each syllable (she even joins both by a small dash in order not to be mixed up). She has no conflict with the reading of 'palos' — four letters for two syllables — but she has conflict with the word 'gallo' which is converted by her into 'gal-lli-na' (hen) in order to have the number of letters coinciding with the number of syllables.

4.3 — There is a conflict between the adjustment of the quantity of letters to the quantitative properties of the referent and the quantity of syllables of the names intended to be written. Example: the experimenter writes GALLO and asks if in order to write 'gallina' it is necessary to have more letters or fewer letters. Mariana answers that we need fewer letters because 'la gallina es maś chica' (the hen is smaller), and she writes GALL. To the question of how one could write 'pollito' (little chicken), Mariana answers 'con las mismas, pero menos' (with the same letters, but fewer) and she writes GAL.

In order to write her own name Mariana asks for four letters (as many as the number of years she has); in order to write her mother's name (that has two syllables) she asks for seven letters, and to write her father's name (also two syllables) she asks 'as much as one thousand!'

Identical syllables do not receive the same representation. Example: The experimenter writes PA and says 'I wrote pa, how could we write papá?', and Mariana adds PA and reads, in agreement with her own hypothesis of two letters for each syllable, 'pa-pá.'

4.6 — One letter for each syllable, but three as a minimum quantity. Example:

MOU 'li-mo-nes' (lemons)

OMR 'pi-ñas' (pineapples)

4.8 — There are conflicts not yet resolved between several hypotheses: attributing one or two letters to each syllable; adjusting the number of letters to the number of syllables of the name; and adjusting the number of letters to the quantitative properties of the referent.

Example: Mariana knows how to write OSO (bear). She's been asked whether "a little ant will have more or less letters," and Mariana answers a very obvious thing, 'Less! Because it is very small! Only two.' She writes two letters, but she reads, in syllables, 'hor-mi . . .' and she adds one then she reads 'hor-mi-ga' and she adds another one; with the four written letters she reads 'hor-mi-gui-ta-' but she gets into conflict when she compares the writings of OSO (bear, three letters) and 'horniguita' (four letters), and she rejects her own writing.

These two evolutions clearly exemplify — in two extreme situations of cultural stimulation — the conflicts of a purely internal nature that emerge spontaneously in the psychogenesis whenever the child tries to understand the writing system. In this domain, like in other domains of cognitive development, to understand implies to assimilate, to transform in order to discover the system of transformations that generate it; it implies to reconstruct, to reinvent.

It seems clear that in order to go from the one-to-one correspondence that we have pointed out (to one syllable, in the order of emission, only one letter, but *any* letter), to a correspondence of another kind, where two similar syllables have a similar representation, it is necessary to have some specific information which can only be provided by the environment. However, this information from the environment enters into the process as a new source of conflicts and not as an immediate solution. When the child attempts to understand the models that are proposed by the environment (and, among them, the child's name in its conventional spelling is the most important of all those models), he or she utilizes his or her own hypotheses. For example, for a child in the period of strict syllabic hypothesis, the total writing of the name is 'unreadable.' Some children try compromise solutions such as this: reading the first name and the family name in the same piece of writing, so that every letter may be interpreted syllabically.

We have no time to show, within the limits of this paper, what type of information is relevant to each step of this evolution, nor what is the type of information that helps the child to go ahead, and what is the type of information that prevents the child from understanding it further, even if the child complains about doing what the school expects him (her) to do.

I have tried to show how difficult and intricate are the ways to establish a relationship between oral language and written language. Children may remain for long periods with the syllabic hypothesis, in spite of very precise pressures of the milieu. In many cases it is only after having explored several ways out of the conflict unsuccessfully that they discover that one has to abandon the syllabic hypothesis, and replace it by an analysis which goes beyond the syllable. Children will not change their minds overnight because they, as scientists do, cling to their hypotheses and are not ready to drop them on the first obstacle in their application. From now on, children are ready to understand the internal rationality of the system. Only at this point do orthography problems start.

It is important to realize that neither the syllabic hypothesis not the criterion of minimum quantity can be attributed to a suggestion of the environment (many articles, conjunctions, prepositions, and pronouns are written with one or two letters in Spanish; parents do not teach that every letter stands for a syllable). Those hypotheses are real constructions built up by children when trying to understand the system of rules that generates writings. With the syllabic hypothesis the child begins to explore new possibilities: the relationship between writing and the formal aspects of speech.

Before this period, the amount of letters either remains fixed or varies, but in accordance with a well-defined parameter. It is not the number of syllables in the word that makes the number of letters increase. Neither is it the opposition word-phrase.

Only the quantitative variations of the quantifiable properties of the object may lead to such a variation (larger in size, older in age, increasing number of elements). It is also very important to realize that children don't ask for a qualitative relationship between letters and referents (such as a similarity between the form of the letters and the object's shape). Generally, quantitative relations have a primacy over the qualitative ones.

What will happen then when children are confronted with texts that are produced and read by some other, texts that are supposed to represent a complete sentence, and not a series of names? I have presented elsewhere an answer to this question (Ferreiro, 1978). I am in a position to confirm what I have then said: There is a period during which the child makes a careful distinction between 'what is written' and 'what could be read.' The reading of a complete sentence does not come, for them, from a text where each one of the words that was pronounced has been written in the order of their utterance. The reading of a complete sentence may come from a text where only the names which have been pronounced are represented. And if there are more pieces of the writing than the number of names that have been pronounced, the child imagines that one has added other names which are compatible with the semantic content of the sentence. Javier and Mariana both present this type of behavior when they are faced with a written sentence that has been read before them: Mariana (4.3) in face of the sentence LA SEÑORA COME PASTEL (the lady eats cake) correctly places 'señora' and 'pastel'; in LA nothing is said because there are not enough letters, and COME, she believes, says 'bebe' (baby) which does not prevent her from accepting that the complete text may be read as 'la señora come pastel' (the lady eats cake) or as — alternative version — 'señora comiendo pastel' (lady eating cake).

Javier (5.2) in DELFINO VENDIÓ TRES GATITOS (Delfino sold three little cats) locates 'Delfino' in the place of the first word and each one of the three small cats in question on the three strings of the remaining letters. This does not prevent him from treating them simultaneously as 'ga-ti-tos' (each of the three strings of letters has, at the same time, a value as a referent and a value as a syllabic representation of the plural name). This does not prevent him either from correctly repeating the sentence that reproduces what the experimenter has pointed out, as if the agreement in this respect was a total one.

'Delfino vendió tres gatitos' is only an adapted version of sentences which have been very well studied in some other experimental studies by us: In Monterrey we used MAMA COMPRÓ TRES TACOS (Mummy bought three tacos) and in Geneva MAMAN PREPARE TROI GATEAUX (Mummy prepares three cakes) in order to specifically study the effect of a sentence where the number of words that were written (four) coincides with the number of objects referred to (mummy and the three tacos or three cakes). In these studies we were able to show the popularity of the interpretation already mentioned. Additional support to the interpretation that — for children at a certain level of conceptualization — only the names are written was obtained in the following way: When one word is taken out, some children think that the result can be read as 'maman prepare deux gateaux' (mummy prepares two cakes); when still another word is taken out the result is 'maman prepare un gateau' (mummy prepares on cake).

When we reach this limit, a new question arises: Is it possible to write 'maman ne prepare pas des gateaux' (mummy does not prepare cakes)? The possibility of writing the negation brings us to another aspect of the relationship between oral and written language: the relationship between the writing and the truth value which is attributed to the utterance to be represented. Falsehood cannot be written; it does not deserve a written representation. This is not said by slum children; it is said by children of the middle class in Geneva, who are permeated by a literate culture that has been created precisely for them and where what can be imagined has no limits. 'Les enfants vont a l'ecole' (children go to school) may be written: This is the opinion of about 90 per cent of children between 4 and 6 years. On the other hand 'la tortue vole' (the turtle flies) cannot be written: This is the opinion of about 70 per cent of the same children. Some small children accept writing a falsehood, but we must look carefully into the 'how' of the proposed solution. Lisandro, 4 years old, without knowing 'officially' how to write, solves the problems of truth and falsehood linked to representation. We write and read before Lisandro the following sentence: UN PAJARO VUELA (a bird flies). Lisandro says, 'I already knew it.' The experimenter (being rather astonished, because she knows that Lisandro does not know how to read) asked what it was that he knew. Lisandro explains: 'Yes, because birds fly, then a bird flies.' A perfect syllogism. It is clear that for Lisandro what we wrote is necessarily true. When we propose to him if it is possible to write 'There are no birds' we are probably asking him to write something that is false. Lisandro answers: 'The letter that there are no birds I have to make it twisted'. There are no birds, because the letters of there are no birds must be twisted. And Lisandro, who only knows how to write a few letters, imposes upon himself — for the sake of internal consistency — the requirement of making letters that are twisted because the other letters do not serve the purpose of representing falsehood.

I have provided some evidence in support of the following assertions:

1 The relations between oral and written language cannot be reduced to the sound-relationship between phoneme and grapheme. They are far more complex.
2 Children go a long and complicated way before discovering that the writing surrounding them is alphabetic in nature. They

explore other hypotheses, some of them not being adequate for the alphabetical system, although they would be appropriate for other systems of writing.

3 The writing that precedes the alphabetical period is far from being unstructured: It provides evidence of children's efforts in the search for an understanding of the laws of the system.

The pedagogic implications cannot be overstated:

— The understanding of the written system seems to imply the construction of a conceptual object (something more than the application of linguistic knowledge or of a metalinguistic reflection to a particular reality). Moreover, reading and writing instruction should take into account the logical problems involved (one-to-one correspondence, relations between the totality and the constituent parts, permutations and combinations, etc.).

— Children have shown to us that they need to reconstruct the written system in order to make it their own. Let us allow them the time and the opportunities for such a tremendous task.

References

BELLEFROID, B. and FERREIRO, E. (1979) 'La segmentation de mots chez l'enfant,' *Archives de Psychologie*, XLVII, 180.

FERREIRO, E. (1978) 'What is written in a written sentence? A developmental answer', *Journal of Education*, 160, 4.

FERREIRO, E., GOMEZ PALACIO, M., GUAJARDO, E., RODRIGUEZ, B., VEGA, A. and CANTU, R.L. (1979) *El nino preescolar y su comprension del sistema de escritura*, Mexico, Direccion General de Educacion especial.

FERREIRO, E. and TEBEROSKY, A. (1979) *Los sistemas de escritura en el desarrollo del nino.* Mexico, Siglo XXI Ed. English translation: (1982) *Literacy before schooling*. Heinemann.

LAVINE, C. (1977) 'Differentiation of letter-like forms in pre-reading children', *Developmental Psychology*, 13, 2.

*Cognitive Processes in Spelling and their Relevance to Spelling Reform**

Uta Frith

Cognitive psychology has flourished on a highly effective, yet astonishingly simple model of how we perceive, remember, think and do things. All these are activities that involve cognitive processes, but most of all, cognitive processes are identified with communication skills. Information processing is the key phrase to characterize this simple model, and it is ideally suited to describe spoken or written language. The model distinguishes between INPUT processes — these could be listening to speech or reading — and OUTPUT processes, such as speaking or writing. In between input and output we have traditionally a 'black box.' Inside we imagine there exists our internal representation of language — and indeed our representation of the world.

This input-output model is also useful in order to consider what we mean by spelling. There are really three subtly, but importantly different meanings of spelling, which are easily confused. If seen in relation to input processes, spelling denotes *orthographic structure*. We can talk of spelling patterns, letter position, specific graphemic units, etc. It is clear that 6 year old beginning readers are already sensitive to orthographic structure (Henderson and Chard, 1980). Even non-readers, for instance, can distinguish illegally spelled words (prtd) from legally spelled ones (prid). It is easy to observe this by asking them to sort out such stimuli into the categories 'possible words' and 'definitely not words.' If seen in relation to output processes, spelling means *word production*. In order to be correct, the word has to be correct letter-by-letter. It is this production process that has received least study and that yet gives rise to more problems than other aspects of literacy. Spelling also sometimes means *spelling knowledge*, which is represented inside the black box, as if in some internal dictionary. How this knowledge is actually acquired and how it is available for use is still largely unknown. An example would be the knowledge we

* Originally printed in *Spelling Progress Bulletin*, 1982.

bring to bear in spelling entirely new words by analogy and in detecting errors in our own writing.

If we go along with the model, these three meanings of 'spelling' have to be kept apart, as quite different psychological processes are involved in the three functions. Spelling as an INPUT skill has most to do with *reading*. Spelling as an OUTPUT skill has most to do with *writing*. The third function of spelling is the least accessible to study and rests largely on inference, while input and output skills can be observed directly. Nevertheless, we cannot do without the assumption that a literate person has a vast store of knowledge about the written forms of words. There must be an internalized system of *visible language* just as there is of spoken language.

One very intriguing question is in what form is this knowledge represented? Is there really something like a collection of specific visual images for every word? That visible language has a 'visual' component must be taken for granted. However, this component is *abstract-visual*, not physical-visual: structures that are not photographs, but like programmes that specify each letter in its correct position, whatever physical shape the letter may have.

The internal representation of spelling knowledge is not as speculative an assumption as it might appear. That the notion has a psychological reality can perhaps be shown by the existence of spelling riddles in folklore. A number of these have been collected and discussed by Green and Pepicello (1980). They classified spelling riddles into several types, two of which are especially relevant here. The first type is like this: 'What's black and white and red/read all over? (a newspaper).' This is concerned with the fact that the same sound can have a different spelling. The sound in context tricks you into thinking of the wrong member of the pair, namely (red) as colour rather than (read) as in reading. This type of riddle belongs to the vast class of jokes that are known as puns. Although puns can be understood without spelling knowledge, one wonders if their enjoyment is not enhanced by the fact that similar sounding words can be written differently.

The second type of riddle is as follows: 'What tune does everyone like?' (fortune) 'What ants are the largest?' (giants) 'What age is served at breakfast?' (sausage) This type is concerned with the fact that the same spelling can have different sounds (for example, *tune* sounds something like 'tchoon' in TUNE, but 'tchin' in FORTUNE). What is interesting about this type of riddle is that it really shows that letter strings are known or represented internally without respect to a specific sound. It is the same /t/u/n/e/ if it is pronounced /tchoon/ or /tchin/'.

These few examples suffice to show that there is some psychological reality to the notion of internal spelling knowledge and that this knowledge rests on a quite complex system of visible language.

Naturally, cognitive psychologists have elaborated the *simple input-*

output model into highly sophisticated versions and excellent accounts are available (for example Cohen, 1977; Morton, 1979; Seymour, 1979). The findings that emerged from experiments based on a cognitive model are very relevant to students of reading and spelling. I believe that they have brought about a significant advance in our under-standing of reading and spelling skills (Frith, 1980). The main advance compared to older studies probably rests in the microanalysis of reading and spelling. The black box has in fact begun to be unpacked.

A specific example is the analysis of reading and spelling skills in terms of two relatively independent strategies. We can read a word — to some extent at least — as if it were a Chinese symbol, that is, disregarding any relationships of letters to speech sounds. Hence this strategy has been termed 'Chinese.' This strategy is very fast, but the problem with it is that every single word needs to have a specific entry in an internal lexicon. If it is a short word, it can be recognized as a whole pattern straight away; if it is a long word, or is inflected, then it needs to be broken down into proper meaningful segments first, each of which are then instantly recognized. The important point is that this is not letter-by-letter reading; the meaningful segments are groups of letters taken in at once. Furthermore, individual letters are not translated into sound. With this 'Chinese' strategy it is therefore quite irrelevant, if the letter-sound correspondences are ambiguous or unpredictable from general rules. We can illustrate this with an example of 'Chinese' reading that is familiar to all of us: seeing '12' or 'XII' makes us say 'twelve', 'zwolf,' 'douze' or 'dodici' according to the language.

The other and truly alphabetic strategy has been termed 'Phoenician.' This strategy treats the alphabetic writing system as it was originally intended by its inventors, the Phoenicians. Letter and speech sound are intimately connected, but in such a way that the stream of speech is broken up into small artificial units which are designated phonemes and which are represented by particular graphemes. To use this strategy, one does not require specific word recognizers: any word can be read — in theory — by pronouncing each letter according to the rules. The problem here for English is that we need to put together the single letters into bigger meaningful units before we can really pronounce them, or to know where to put the stress (Smith, 1980. For the most part this is not the fault of the orthography, but the 'fault' of the spoken language itself. Phonemes do change in context. Hence we have problems with, for example, finite-infinite, active-action, courage-courageous. Here the same vowel in the word pairs is pronounced very differently, but spelled the same. This orthographic convention makes transparent the underlying relationship of the words — in spite of the fact that our speech (at present) does not make such a relationship very clear. The examples also serve to illustrate that written language is not merely parasitic on spoken language — rather it makes an independent contribution to communication. Indeed, it may itself affect speech and can be shown in numerous examples even to have changed speech over time (Levitt, 1978).

The two reading strategies, 'Chinese' and 'Phoenician' are well known to teachers by the labels 'Look-and-say' and 'Phonics.' Both have been applied to reading as well as to spelling, but there is some indication that 'Phoenician' has more affinity to spelling. One reason for saying this is that reading errors are usually not mispronunciations of component sounds, but an error is usually a completely different word that is substituted. It seems that the wrong lexical entry was being activated, rather than that a string of sounds was laboriously and falsely marked out. On the other hand, spelling errors and slips of the pen are very often phonetic, that is, they do seem to be derived by an application of sound-to-letter rules. Marsh *et al.* (1981) compared errors in reading and spelling the same material in three age groups and concluded that the strategies were markedly different.

Even good spellers make spelling errors, usually by accident rather than by ignorance. Interestingly enough, many of their unintentional slips of the pen are in homophonic words, for example, *their* for *there*, *to* for *too*, etc. Two aspects of these slips are important: that they are words themselves and that they sound similar to the target word. Since word is substituted by word, probably a confusion between two automatic spelling programmes occurred. Since the correct sound is retained, it appears that the spelling program was retrieved through sound. Morton (1980) suggests that a phonological code could be used as a unit to access the letter-by-letter code for the word. The mental lexicon itself may be organized phonologically (Fay and Cutler, 1977). Thus the direct ('Chinese') or lexical route still may be triggered by a phonological code. However, its role would not be to provide phoneme to grapheme correspondences, only to retrieve an automatic spelling program for a whole word. Why should a sound code rather than a visual code take on this role?

A theory that is relevant to this notion has been proposed by O'Connor and Hermelin (1978). According to their theory, there is an affinity of temporal-sequential processes (which include speaking and spelling) with phonological coding. Thus, while writing, sound is the appropriate code and would override a visual code, and, as in speech, does not distinguish for instance, *their* from *there* (Frith and Frith, 1980). In contrast, in reading, a visual code would seem highly appropriate. It is a very fast process, where sound enters at a later stage only. It can readily be imagined that if there was a race between 'Chinese' and 'Phoenician' word recognition, the Chinese one would win. On the other hand, in writing this speed is not necessarily an advantage as the writing process itself is slow enough for a sound code to catch up easily.

Evidence for the separation of reading and writing strategies is also available from another source. In young children just beginning to learn to read and write, Bryant and Bradley (1980) observed that they would read words they could not write and write words they could not read. This odd discrepancy was explained by the fact that the children spontaneously preferred to read words by Look-and-say, but to write them by Phonics. The important observation that young pre-school children may take quite readily to writing, given basic knowledge of letter names and sounds, was analyzed by Charles Read (1971). He also found that often such precocious children could not read what they themselves had written. To decode sound to letter seemed more 'natural' than to decode letter to sound.

Discrepancies between reading and writing should not come as a surprise. Indeed, they are expected in terms of an information processing model, since input and output are not just the same process in reverse, but are in fact quite independent of each other. Using a computer analogy, the information typed in at the keyboard terminal bears only a superficial relationship to what appears on the print-out. The information that is typed in can be, but need not be, converted into signals that activate a printer. The speeds of the various operations involved also are independent of each other. The printing time is presumably limited by mechanical conditions specific to the printer. Similarly, writing or typing by hand cannot be faster than the motor system allows.

This notion of independence of input and output has important implications for teaching and for changing spelling. It implies that learning to read does not at the same time necessarily lead to learning to spell. Furthermore, as already mentioned, input and output processes seem to have specific preferences for particular codes. For example, a lexical recognition might rely on a 'visual' code, a sound-letter translation system may well rely on a sound-based code. A sound-based code, as O'Connor and Hermelin have suggested, is essentially a sequential code; a visual code on the other hand is a spatial code that is not dependent on temporal sequence. In reading, we can imagine that a spatial code is efficient. In spelling, a sequential code might be especially advantageous, as it goes along with sequential programmes.

All this supports the idea that the requirements for input (reading) and for output (writing) processes are not only independent, but in some sense incompatible. It seems as if the Phoenician invention of the alphabet is tailor-made for writing, while the Chinese system is tailor-made for reading.

One particular difference regards flexibility and rigidity of the processes. It seems to me that flexibility is desirable where processing of input is concerned, simply because the form of the input can vary so much. Material to be read does come in many different forms: prints vary, even given perfect legibility, but legibility also varies, depending on the conditions of, for example, light, distance, state of the material, etc. The idiosyncracies of the sender of the communication may have to be taken into account, his handwriting and his spelling ability. It pays, therefore, for an input processing system to be flexible and adjustable to the situational demands. This is the opposite of having a pre-programmed system, where we would utterly depend on input material being reliably the same in every case. I would like to suggest that this sort of system is not viable for reading, but is very well suited for an output process, such as writing.

For output processes to function efficiently, pre-programming is needed. This requires a fixed sequence of actions. Preprogramming is evident in handwriting — which is characteristic of each individual. There may be a number of quite long automatic sequences for frequent words and frequent word-components. Studies are in progress that look at the exact timing of writing movements in order to discover the size of basic units as well as longer spelling programs. It is important, however, to realize that spelling programs do not reside in the actual writing movements. This would be absurd, since we can spell equally well if we type, or print, or write with our non-preferred hand, or spell orally. The spelling program underlies the motor program, but is not identical to it. It is true that we still know little about the nature of the output programmes, and we also know very little about the input programmes, but experimentation is following along quite promising paths. It is clear that what appears to be a superficially simple relationship of spelling and reading processes is in fact not at all simple.

What conclusions can we draw at this point that might have some bearing on spelling reform issues? It seems to me that any reform that is guided by a single principle, if it is an advantage to one process, it is bound to be a disadvantage to the other. A single principle cannot satisfy both processes. If we take the principle of unambiguous letter-sound correspondence, it may well be that spelling would benefit by a simplified sound-based system, but, inevitably, reading would suffer. Fluent reading is not primarily a sound-based process, but much more a visual one and could be simultaneous rather than sequential. Writing must always be sequential, in contrast.

In recognizing words we can actually benefit from an orthographic system such as the present one where information is presented at many different linguistic levels. There is a lot of redundancy in the conventional spelling of many words, which enables us, if we wish, to learn about, for example, the word's language origin, the word's prior pronunciation, the word's form class, or its relationship to other words. Visible language, as I have already pointed out, is not just a derivative version or imperfect reflection of spoken language. Language is more than speech and has many more aspects than sound. Although there is slow but continuous change in both domains of written and spoken language, it is not clear who or what exactly controls the change. If we knew we would presumably be on the way towards an optimal orthographic system. Clearly, as an experimental psychologist, I would prefer to understand the psychological processes underlying reading and spelling, before trying to change them. Nevertheless, I would like to make a suggestion that is based on the study of cognitive processes. This study taught us that the ideal orthography is different if seen from the point of view of the reader, and the writer. Instead of trying to achieve a compromise — which I believe is actually the continuous state of English orthography — we might look for a radical alternative with help from computer technology. All we need is a translator device (our 'black box') that mediates between the ideally efficient sender and the receiver of the written message. The sender, if he likes the Phoenician style, could write in his own preferred system, possibly in shorthand. The reader (if he likes the Chinese style) could read the message in as non-phonetic and as redundant a way as he liked. The 'black box' would have stored all necessary spelling programs. As recent work by Colin Brooks and Robert Baker presented at this conference shows, such a solution is not as Utopian as it sounds. What makes this technological solution especially exciting to me is that it seems backed by theory and results from cognitive studies in spelling. I hope therefore that it can cut through the tangled controversy of pros and cons of spelling reform and provide a new alternative of communicating in visible language.

References

BRYANT, P.E. and BRADLEY, L. (1980). 'Why children sometimes write words which they do not read,' in FRITH, U. (Ed.) *Cognitive Processes in Spelling*, London, Academic Press.

COHEN, G. (1977). *The Psychology of Cognition*, London, Academic Press.

FAY, D. and CUTLER, A. (1977), 'Malapropisms and the structure of the mental lexicon', *Linguistic Inquiry*, 8, pp. 505–20.

FRITH, U. (Ed.) (1980). *Cognitive Processes in Spelling,* London, Academic Press.

FRITH, U. and FRITH, C.D. (1980). 'Relationship between reading and spelling', in KAVANAGH, J.F. and VENEZKY, R.L. (Eds), *Orthography, Reading and Dyslexia,* Baltimore, University Park Press.

GREEN, T.A. and PEPICELLO, W.J. (1980). 'Sight and spelling riddles. *Journal of American Folklore*, 93, pp. 23–34.

HENDERSON, L. and CHARD, J. (1980). 'The reader's implicit knowledge of orthographic structure', in FRITH, U. (Ed.) *Cognitive Processes in Spelling*, London, Academic Press.

LEVITT, J. (1978). 'The influence of orthography on phonology: A comparative study' (English, French, Spanish, Italian, German), *Linguistics,* 208, pp. 43–67.

MARSH, G., FRIEDMAN, M., DESBERG, P. and SATERDAHL, K. (1981). Comparison of reading and spelling strategies in normal and reading disabled children', in FRIEDMAN, M., DAS, J.P. and O'CONNOR, N. (Eds) *Intelligence and Learning*, New York, Plenum Press.

MORTON, J. (1979). 'Word recognition', in MORTON, J and MARSHALL, J.C. (Eds). *Psycholinguistics, Series II,* London, Elek.

MORTON, J. (1980). 'The logogen model and orthographic structure', in FRITH, U. (Ed.), *Cognitive Processes in Spelling*, London, Academic Press.

O'Connor, N. and Hermelin, B. (1978). *Seeing and Hearing and Space and Time*, London, Academic Press.

Read, C. (1971). 'Preschool children's knowledge of English phonology'. *Harvard Educational Review*, 41, pp. 1–34.

Seymour, P.H.K. (1979). *Human Visual Cognition*, London, Collier Macmillan.

Smith, P.T. (1980). 'Linguistic information in spelling', in Frith, U. (Ed.). *Cognitive Processes in Spelling*, London, Academic Press.

Writing and Reading: A Marriage between Equals

Jennifer E. Barr

Introduction

> The Male Chauvinist Empire is crumbling — not just in the face of Feminist opposition but in the face of economic realities . . . the traditional stereotype of men as 'strong dominant providers' is cracking and a major male identity crisis has arrived'. (Phillip Hodson in *Men: An Investigation into the Emotional Male*)

Sex and role stereotypes rarely change as a result of careful, analytical thinking. Rather, they are honed and hewn by what is actually happening in society: as experience reveals that on·occasion the strong are less than strong, the weak are less than weak, perceptions change and with them the subtle fabric of thinking that governs our expectations and assumptions. The process need not be destructive — Hodson's thesis (1984) is that the changes in the way in which women are viewed in society has led to a reappraisal of the male role, and this in turn has opened the door to a consideration of important but neglected aspects of male psychology, such as the role and place of emotion. The sadness is that such an examination might not have begun, had it not been for the impetus of the women's movement.

The purpose of this chapter is to argue the thesis that over the past ten years the status of the reading process has similarly undergone a subtle redefinition in the face of developments in our understanding of the *other* processes involved in the language arts. No longer can reading be held to occupy a solitary pedestal, served and serviced by the skills of listening, speaking, writing and thinking. Yet to imply that reading has been dethroned is not to imply that it has been discredited, for it is argued that it is only through a proper understanding of the various skills of the language arts, together with an acknowledgement and appreciation of their mutual interdependence, that the value and potential of these skills for aiding development in the learner can be fully realised.

Jennifer E. Barr

Reading and Writing: Two Studies

In the preceding chapter, Frith has argued that at the level of the *word*, the processes of reading and spelling (input and output) are functionally independent. Reading, however, is more than barking at print, and writing more than producing a fair and correct copy of text. To what extent is there an overlap in the higher order skills involved in reading and writing, and what strategies can be used in the classroom to develop these abilities? It is of interest that in recent years two studies have been conducted in Britain which have used a similar methodology to ask the same questions about the learning process, the one from the perspective of reading *The Effective Use of Reading* (Lunzer and Gardner, 1979) the other from the perspective of writing *Writing Matters across the Curriculum* (Spencer, 1983). Both studies look at the issues as they affect the young teenager, and include surveys of current practice in school and interviews with teachers; both suggest and develop activities which could be used to promote development of these higher order skills and both found it necessary in the research report to preface their findings with a discussion of the wider context of literacy and its relation to speaking and listening. The principal common issues arising from these two studies will be discussed briefly.

One of the main findings to emerge from both studies is that there is a conflict of educational goals in our schools, between on the one hand the imparting of knowledge and on the other, developing in pupils the willingness and ability to reflect. The surveys of current practice in the various subject departments of the secondary school reveal that *most* reading which occurs in school serves the first goal and takes the form of short-burst reading; similarly most writing consists of dictation, notes and short answers to questions. Both sets of researchers warn of the danger that excessive use of rote methods can engender a rote approach to learning and a tendency towards passive absorption of facts. In addition, constant simplification of the text can result in a loss of meaning which will further inhibit the pupil's interest in interrogating the material which is being handled.

As an alternative approach, the two studies argue for the active engagement of the pupil in his learning and for approaches to reading and writing through the subject areas of the curriculum which will develop and foster reflective thinking. Spencer (1983) speaks of 'Learning to write or writing to learn?' (p. 6) and Lunzer and Gardner (1979) quote from a school policy document entitled 'Learning to Read and Reading to Learn' (p. 276). Only if the pupil is encouraged to think about and work with materials and ideas freely in a wide range of informal situations, will he be able to use and develop his existing literacy skills as genuine tools for learning, and so pave the way for greater success and satisfaction as a thinker.

> Writing is a search for meaning involving both excitement of mind and emotion *and* awareness of language as the manipulable means of achieving and conveying meaning. (Spencer, 1983, p. 142)

> Reading for learning becomes a 'conversation with the text' in which the student asks his own questions, finds the answers and makes his own comment. (Lunzer and Gardner, 1979, p. 303)

In neither study is it suggested that fostering these skills will be an easy task. What is clear, however, is that the skills can and should be fostered, and not just as an optional extension once the 'basic' lower-order skills have been mastered. Using literacy for learning is the context which gives meaning and purpose to the acquisition of the mechanical skills and the challenge for teaching is to offer opportunities and strategies for the simultaneous development of a wide range of skills, through a combination of guided practice and the provision of genuine learning situations.

> There are methods of study which refine our purposeful search of the printed text. (Lunzer and Gardner, 1979, p. 301)

> A key idea is that qualities in a piece of writing — such as accuracy, conciseness, organisation — are the results of certain kinds of thinking. Teaching consists in arranging things so that the appropriate kinds of thinking occur. (Spencer, 1983, p. 143)

Reading and Writing — Fostering a Common Learning

It would appear that these two studies, conducted independently and in two different educational systems, arrive at broadly the same conclusion: to the extent that reading and writing are tools for cognitive activity they foster similar goals and call for a similar level of active involvement on the part of the learner. The processes are linked at a more fundamental level, however, for both deal with *text*, and both can therefore foster the type of extended thinking that is only possible through the more formal medium of written language (Barr, 1983). Speech may be more flexible, more responsive to feedback from the listener, more colourful and variable in terms of accent, dialect and patterns of individual usage (Weigl, 1978; Harris and Kay, 1981) but it cannot communicate long-term and long distance. Written language, by contrast, is unsupported by a shared context between writer and reader: the communication must be self-sufficient and self-explanatory, carrying its meaning through linguistic elements alone. References and relationships cannot be implied, they must be explicitly stated and logically entailed, and the language used is accordingly more formal and impersonal. As Wilkinson and his colleagues (1980) describe it, written language is an 'extended and shaped construction' (p. 215). The benefits are clear for the reader, who has the power to manipulate the material, to attend selectively, to skip forward, to refer back, to move in his own time and at his own pace (Smith, 1982). There are benefits also for the writer, who has similar scope to work at his own rate, back-referencing and anticipating, revising and rewriting (Byrne, 1979).

> Writing, because of its amenability to storage, review and revision, makes possible a kind of extended and involved thought that is almost impossible without writing. (Bereiter, 1980, p. 88)

Perhaps this point is most clearly expressed in the question posed by E M Forster:

> 'How do I know what I think until I see what I say?' (quoted in Shaughnessy, 1977, p. 79)

For the young learner who is seeking to master the formalities of written language, there are many concepts about print which must be grasped, for example, that there is a distinction between drawings and text, the one representing objects, the other carrying a message (Goodman, 1982); that letters represent sounds and can be built into words (Ferreiro and Teberosky, 1983); that there are spatial demands of text and particular ways of attending and orienting to printed language (Clay, 1975). As Payton and Ferreiro have illustrated in chapters of this book and elsewhere:

> Internalization of the complexities of print is an intricate and lengthy process in which the child has consistently initiated and sustained cognitive activity. (Payton, 1982, p. 73)

The point which is of relevance here is that these concepts are concerned with the characteristics of *print*, and as such have equal relevance for understanding both the processes of reading and of writing.

Reading and Writing: A Separation of the Processes

Thus far it has been argued that many of the concepts about print which must be mastered by the language learner apply to reading and writing alike; indeed, textual language itself fosters a type of thinking that may be explored equally through either process. It is for this reason that the application of a concept such as 'cohesion', the influence of text semantics (Halliday and Hasan, 1976) can be developed either through examination of the activity of the fluent reader (Goodman, 1982; Lewis, 1982) or of the writer (Harris and Kay, 1981).

Despite evidence of much common ground, the question must still be asked, to what extent do reading and writing require the development and application of *different* higher order skills? It has been shown by Frith in the previous chapter that, despite the fact that reading and writing operate on a common orthography, when handling individual words quite different strategies may be used for encoding and decoding in order to maximize the information available for the particular task in hand. Thus, in reading (where the goal is recognition of the intended word and efficient access of its meaning) a whole word strategy may be used; in spelling (where attention to detail is crucial) a letter by letter approach may be adopted. A similar argument may be developed for the operation of the higher order skills: to the extent that there are differences between the goals of fluent reading and extended writing, there will be different strategies adopted and different foci of attention. The purposes of 'reading to learn' are varied — the reader must bring his existing knowledge to bear on the text, question the text to extract the author's intended meaning and form his own judgment on the communication offered. In 'writing to learn' the focus is altered, for it is the *writer* who possesses the message and the intention to communicate, and his task is to find form and vocabulary that will adequately express that message and convey it to the unknown reader. The reader need pay attention to the style and characteristics of the writing only in so far as they contribute to the substance of what is being said; the writer ignores them at his peril, for they are his very pass-key to success as a communicator.

Just as at the level of the individual word, so the higher order processes of reading and writing appear to be functionally independent. The focus of the learner's attention and his concern for such features as style, grammar and form will vary depending on whether the task requires the extraction of meaning or the expression of meaning. Reading and writing may share the common medium of text, and they may share a common potential for developing reflective thought, but as procedures for handling textual language they are fundamentally and functionally distinct.

It is not just between reading and writing that such a distinction operates. Even within the writing act, there are processes that can conflict:

> Even a casual analysis makes it clear that the number of things that must be dealt with simultaneously in writing is stupendous: handwriting, spelling, punctuation, word choice, syntax, textual connections, purpose, organisation, clarity, rhythm, euphony, the possible reactions of various readers and so on. To pay conscious attention to all of these would overload the information-processing capacity of the most towering intellects. (Scardamalia in Bereiter, 1980, p. 89)

If each of the aspects of writing listed by Scardamalia could be processed without affecting the others, the act of writing would still be highly complex and demanding. The picture, however, is still more complicated, particularly for the young writer: Laberge and Samuels

(1974) have considered a theory of automatic information processing and concluded that voluntary attention may be necessary for processing at first, but it becomes less necessary as automaticity is achieved. In addition, the general information processing capacity of young writers is limited: they cannot process simultaneously information at a number of levels if conscious attention to the processing is required.

It is here that a tension between such processes as spelling and composing can arise: if conscious attention is required for spelling, then composition is likely to suffer. Collins and Gentner (1980) describe the problem as one of 'downsliding', a tendency to be pulled into lower and more local levels of task processing at the expense of the higher level relationships. This is less of a problem for older children, who not only will have developed a greater processing capacity, but will also have achieved a degree of mastery over the lower levels of processing, allowing them to spend more resources coordinating ideas. Nevertheless, simultaneous attention to the processes of composition and transcription can be mutually interfering, a realization which led Smith (1982) in *Writing and the Writer* to pronounce:

> The rule is simple: composition and transcription must be separated and transcription must come last. (p. 24)

Separate Processes: A Case for Celibacy?

In developing his thesis, Smith draws on the picture of the businessman 'composing' into his dictaphone, and the secretary 'transcribing' once the process of composition is complete — separate and distinct processes best developed in isolation.

It is here, however, that a fundamental paradox becomes apparent. Few young writers have the luxury of a dictaphone and secretary, and even the adoption of a procedure such as drafting and redrafting to encourage selective attention to the various features of the writing can only partially separate the processes of composition and transcription. At the heart of the paradox lies the issue that you learn to spell by spelling:

> Learning to spell takes time; it begins with misspellings. (Smith, 1982, p. 185)

Thus Bissex's young son Paul could develop in his early years a simplified system of orthography which would allow him to communicate in writing without having first to master all the complexities of English orthography (Bissex, 1980). Over the years, however, through the joint influences of reading and further testing in writing, Paul's personal system became refined in the direction of Standard English. Thus at the age of five Paul could write 'drakthens' for 'directions', at 7 this was refined to 'direkshons' and by 8 years he could write 'directions' and know with confidence that he was correct.

> What is learned in one language encounter becomes data for further predictions in other encounters. (Wilson, 1981, p. 89)

In the case of spelling, what is learned in word study and reading becomes data for further prediction in word production and writing. When writing then, as when reading, children act as hypothesis-testers, forming predictions about word and sentence structure, assimilating and applying knowledge in a variety of language situations. The foundations for skill acquisition may be laid through an isolation of the processes of writing (for example in the spelling lesson) but full mastery can only be achieved and demonstrated when these skills are reintegrated in the natural context of language production, and where simultaneous processing can be achieved at several different levels in the course of fluent and purposeful writing. In the case of this example, transcription and composition each have their own identity but they find their true selves in acknowledging and expressing their mutual interdependence.

This paradox underlies work in every area of the language arts. The processes of fluent reading and extended writing may be separate and distinct but they are developed through a lively and sustained interaction. As Smith (1982) explains, you learn to read for meaning by reading with the mind of the writer; you learn to write to communicate, by writing with the eye of a reader.

Such flexible posturing has always been possible in relation to text and it is used by successful writers who are only too aware that the message can take on a life which is independent of the original intention of the writer. This is nowhere better illustrated than in the following example. Goethe had the experience of reading as an old man a verse which he had etched on the wall of a mountain hut forty years earlier. To Goethe as a young writer, the verse was a simple celebration of peace. To Goethe as an old man it spoke of death — and he wept.

In the studies by Lunzer and Gardner, and Spencer cited earlier, a variety of approaches are suggested to help in developing skills of reading and writing for learning. Each relies on a combination of approaches: for example, knowledge of the writing process can be developed through sensitive reading and appreciation of literature; skills in reading for meaning can be developed through flexible use of diagrams and note-taking. The value of combination approaches to work in the language arts is further endorsed in the two sets of Language Arts Guidelines produced by Fife Regional Council Education Committee, which draw heavily on speaking and listening (in addition to reading and writing) in the development of reflective thinking:

> Speaking, writing, reading and listening are very closely intertwined and lend support and encouragement to one another.

Thus, activities designed to foster skills in *reading* may follow examination of text with such varied tasks as discussion, completion of a sequential activity or the production of a diagram, writing, art or drama work. Binns' (1980) extended version of the *writing* process suggests the value of combining the following activities: exploratory talk/reflection/jotting notes/production of a draft/reading, revising, correcting/production of a fair and final copy/reading, reflecting, correcting.

Summary and Conclusions

This chapter has examined the position of reading within the language arts and the argument has been developed on two fronts. On the one hand, there is a plea for the equality of the language arts: no single skill has pre-eminence over the others and each in its own way can be a powerful tool in the development of reflective thinking. There is, therefore, no stable, solitary pedestal for reading. The second strand of argument continues the line of thinking and examines the paradox that while the various processes of language may be separate and distinct, they are best developed through lively and sustained interaction one with the other. You learn to read by reading as a writer, and to write by writing as a reader. To conclude the analogy:

> 'If you would understand men, study women'. (French proverb)

The plea is not for occasional dialogue, or even for uneasy cohabitation. What is advocated is a full and healthy marriage — a marriage between equals!

References

BARR, J.E. (1983) *Spelling in the Context of Writing for a Purpose* unpublished PhD thesis, University of Birmingham.

BEREITER, C. (1980) 'Development in writing' in GREGG, L.W. and STEINBERG, E.R. (Eds) *Cognitive Processes in Writing* Hillsdale, NJ, Erlbaum.

BINNS, R. (1980) 'A technique for developing written language' in CLARK, M.M. and GLYNN, T. *Reading and Writing for the Child with Difficulties*, Educational Review, Occasional Publication No. 8, University of Birmingham.

BISSEX, G.L. (1980) *Gnys at Wrk: A Child Learns to Read and Write*, Cambridge, Mass, Harvard University Press.

BYRNE, D. (1979) *Teaching Writing Skills*, London, Longman.

CLAY, M.M. (1975) *What Did I Write?*, Auckland, Heinemann.

COLLINS, A. and GENTNER, D. (1980) 'A framework for a cognitive theory of writing in GREGG, L.W. and STEINBERG, E.R. (Eds) *Cognitive Processes in Writing* Hillsdale, NJ, Erlbaum.

FERREIRO, E. and TEBEROSKY, A. (1983) *Literacy Before Schooling* London, Heinemann.

GOODMAN, K.S. (1982) *Language and Literacy. The Selected Writings of . . . Volume 1: Process, Theory, Research*, edited by GOLLASCH, F.V. Boston, Routledge and Kegan Paul.

HALLIDAY, M.A.K. and HASAN, R. (1976) *Cohesion in English*, London, Longman.

HARRIS, J. and KAY, S. (1981) *Writing Development: Suggestions for a Policy 8–13*, Metropolitan Borough of Rotherham.

HODSON, P. (1984) *Men: An Investigation of the Emotional Male* Ariel Books, BBC.

LABERGE, D. and SAMUELS, S.J. (1974) 'Toward a Theory of Automatic Information Processing in Reading', *Cognitive Psychology*, 69, pp. 293–323.

LEWIS, G.E. (1982) 'Text structure, text processing and testing reading,' *Midland Association for Linguistic Studies*, 7, pp. 43–69.

LUNZER, E. and GARDNER, K. (1979) *The Effective Use of Reading*, Heinemann Educational Books for the Schools Council.

PAYTON, S. (1982) *Readiness for Reading as an Aspect of Language Growth*, unpublished MEd dissertation, Faculty of Education, University of Birmingham.

SHAUGHNESSY, M.P. (1977) *Errors and Expectations*, Oxford, Oxford University Press.

SMITH, F. (1982) *Writing and the Writer*, London, Heinemann.

SPENCER, E. (1983) *Writing Matters Across the Curriculum*, Scottish Council for Research in Education.

WEIGL, E., (1978) 'Schriftsprache ist Mehr als Lesen und Schreiben, *Grundschule*, 10, pp. 296–8.

WILKINSON, A., BARNSLEY, G., HANNA, P., and SWAN, M. (1980) *Assessing Language Development*, Oxford University Press.

WILSON, M.J. (1981) 'A review of recent research on the integration of reading and writing', *The Reading Teacher*, 34, pp. 896–901.

Part 4. The Language of Print

Introduction

The first article in this section by Merritt is based on a paper which he gave at a conference of the United Kingdom Reading Association in the late sixties and which was published under the title, *The Intermediate Skills*. At that time there was a great deal of discussion on the relative merits of different approaches to the initial teaching of reading. The relative importance of 'primary' skills (the mechanics of reading) and 'higher' level skills (comprehension or thinking in the context of print) and of different stages in the process of learning to read were topics of discussion and of controversy among those concerned with reading. Merritt coined the term 'intermediate skills' to represent important skills and strategies that language users bring to the task of prediction in the context of print. These are based on 'our familiarity with patterns and possibilities — our ability to anticipate what is most likely to follow, or fit any particular sequence or structure'. In the revised paper in the current publication, as in the previous paper, he utilizes a variety of examples to show how effectively we are able to process with the aid of such strategies even when the print is considerably distorted. An appreciation of the full range of skills that fluent language users can bring to the reading situation is important if the teacher is to ensure that the selected approach and chosen materials are such as to enable the learners to utilize all possible resources. Such an awareness is also important for an understanding of the difficulties faced by the less competent language user, and also by children learning to read in a language in which they are not 'at home' (perhaps because it is not their mother tongue). Merritt stresses the importance of recognizing that there are natural opportunities for developing and extending intermediate skills and that it is thus 'a pity to invent artificial strategies'.

The second contribution in this section by Pearce is reprinted here as it appeared in 1972. At that time the terms 'literate', 'semi-literate' and 'illiterate' were frequently identified with reading ages on conventional reading tests (reading ages of over 9 years of age, 7–9, and less than 7 years of age representing the levels referred to above). In this context children seen to have difficulties and 'withdrawn' for remedial help were often thought to have an adequate level of competence when they could achieve a reading age of $8\frac{1}{2}$–9 years. It was already being argued that the above level could not be regarded as sufficient and that a higher reading age was necessary. Within that context Pearce took the title for his paper as 'Literacy is not enough' as a means of exploring the necessity, not so much for a higher reading age, but rather for an appreciation of the skills and strategies not tapped by a reading test, or even required in most texts 'contrived' for the purpose of teaching children to read. The range of features of print with which children must contend in natural text, narrative and information text, is discussed. These include features such as the presentation of the print, the structure of the sentences and the relationship between sentences. This analysis highlights some of the difficulties faced by children in the secondary schools whose prior experience of print has been limited or confined to 'contrived', vocabulary and sentence controlled text. It also provides a useful framework within which to analyze the selection of textbooks which confront the child transferring to the secondary school.

The final contribution to this section, the article by Lewis, which was written for this publication, provides a review of the literature which is now extensive on communication through text. Lewis distinguishes between the *context* within which the reading takes place, 'the strategies, expectations and knowledge' of the reader and the *co-text* of the surrounding text. Evidence is presented to show the importance for any understanding of the process of reading and its cognitive complexity, of appreciating the ongoing nature of comprehension and that the surface form is only a starting point. Meaning, as he shows cannot be 'additive'. 'The meaning' of any text unit can be greater or lesser than the sum of its parts, or in some cases, different'. This paper introduces the reader to a new range of contributors to our understanding of the discourse of printed text. It also highlights the importance of their insights for understanding the full significance of the task in which children and adults are dynamically engaged when processing text and enjoying written narrative. The implications of these findings for reading are explored including the need for integration of skills, transferability from one context to another; the importance of use of genuine text and the ongoing nature of comprehension. The message in that paper (and in the others in this publication also) is that teaching reading should be seen as 'exploratory, an ever-changing adventure, rather than a recipe with few ingredients'.

The Intermediate Skills Revisited

John E. Merritt

Word recognition and comprehension seem to provide a reasonable starting point for any teacher who wishes to look at ways of developing reading skills. This particular distinction is not so convenient or clear cut as it seems, however, and it is one that has helped to sustain a debate that has gone on until well past its bedtime. This is the so-called 'Great Debate' (Chall, 1967) about the relative value of phonic versus whole-word approaches in the early stages of learning to read.

On the phonic side, it was always taken for granted that the main requirement for word recognition is a knowledge of letters and how they relate to sounds. For some, this is essentially a process of 'word building' — a matter of assembling a set of parts according to rules in order to discover what the total assembly amounts to. Others, as a matter of emphasis, teach phonic generalizations by encouraging children to look for the common elements in word families — analysis, rather than synthesis. Few of those who emphasize phonics are so naive, of course, as to argue that comprehension is unimportant in learning to recognize words. Nor do most phonic advocates believe in teaching phonics as a mindless drill. They do assume, however, that learning to read is most efficient when letters, sounds, letter-sound relationships and spelling patterns are systematically taught by one means or another. On the whole-word side, it is taken for granted that language experience and meaning provide the best way in to word recognition and that each word is most efficiently learned as a complete unit — preferably in some meaningful context. Naturally, no teacher supporting this approach would simply ignore letters, sounds and spellings. Nevertheless, the main emphasis in teaching word recognition in the early stages would be on the whole word rather than the separate parts. If we focus too much attention on individual letters, the whole-word enthusiast would argue, the child won't see the wood for the trees.

Whatever the particular mix of phonics and whole word methods, it used to be taken for granted that there are two major aspects to the reading process. On the one hand, there are the separate visual elements or units which children must learn to recognize on sight — either letters, or whole words — which demand one set of skills. On the other hand there are meanings to be extracted — a rather different kind of process which involves other kinds of skills.

The first set of skills seems to represent the mechanics of reading — 'primary' skills if you like. This seems plausible because we have all had the experience of reading something quickly and fluently then realizing that we have read 'mechanically' and not taken in a word. The second set of skills relates to the whole point and purpose of reading — some kind of 'higher order' skills. This, in effect, is thinking in the context of print.

Leaving aside the sometimes rather heated controversies, a great deal of wisdom has in fact been demonstrated by protagonists on both sides of the debate for well over 100 years about how best to develop both sets of skills harmoniously so that each facilitates the other (Huey, 1908; Schonell, 1956). This paper is intended to clarify the nature of this desired interaction between primary skills and higher order skills by outlining a modified version of an argument that was first presented by the author in the late 1960s (Merritt, 1969 and 1970).

In the 1950s and 1960s there was a great surge of linguistic and psycholinguistic research, inspired to no small extent by Miller (1951), that led me to coin the term 'intermediate skills'. This particular term was selected because the skills that were then coming into sharper focus seemed to provide the required bridge between word recognition and comprehension. The nature of these intermediate skills is so obvious — now that research has clarified it — that no teacher need have any worries about understanding them. Indeed, they have been reflected in most teachers' actual practices since time immemorial. They are simply based upon our familiarity with patterns and possibilities — *our ability to anticipate what is most likely to follow, or fit, any particular sequence or structure.*

To illustrate these very simple yet powerful skills notice how easily you can cope with all the flaws in the following text:

> It is surpris---ly easy to read words and sent---es even when
> parts of letters, wh le l tters, gr ps of lett , and even
> ____ words ____ been missed out —
> Wee kan yven red weardz wich ar knot speld kurektly ferle
> ezily of thu lettuz folo at lecet sum of thu 'roolz' — such
> as 'of' sez 'if' bycoz 'o' sez 'i' as in 'wo̲men'.

In reading this passage we obviously react at a number of linguistic levels simultaneously. At any one point we can anticipate what letters or sounds are most likely to occur at a particular point in a word, what the form or class may be for a word in a particular position in a phrase, and what range of possible meanings a word may have within a particular sentence or passage. And what is more, we don't need to be experts in linguistics to be able to do it! We do it without even thinking about it.

It is interesting, however, to see just why these skills are so tremendously powerful in operation, and why, therefore, we need to avoid clumsy teaching strategies which may interfere with their normal, smooth operation.

Why is Anticipation so Powerful in Helping us to Read?

Imagine, for the sake of simple illustration, that you have written every word in your vocabulary in the box illustrated in Figure 1.

Figure 1.

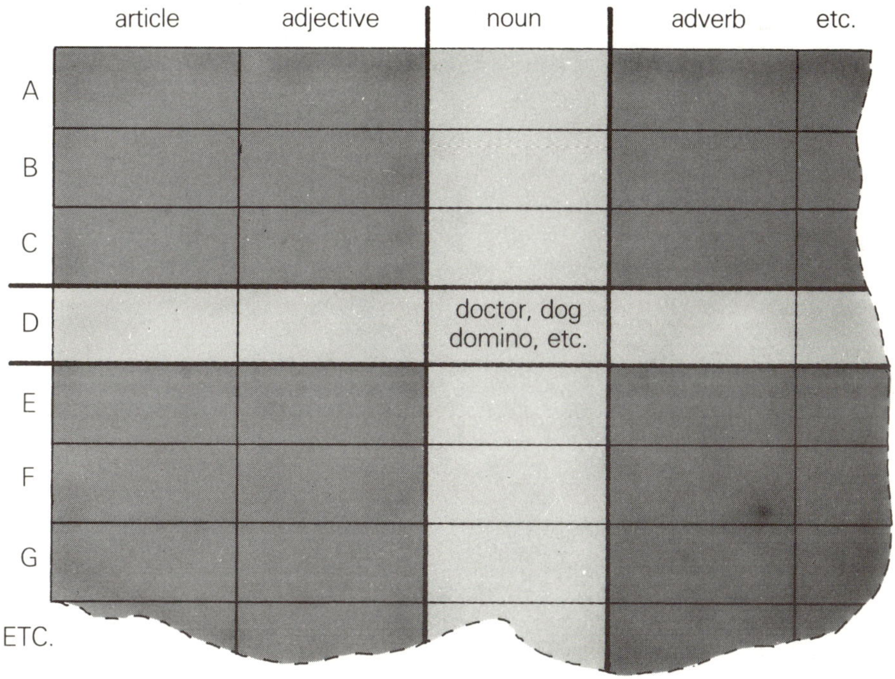

Imagine, also, that you have sorted all these words out in rows and columns, first according to initial letter, then according to part of speech, i.e., verbs, adjectives and so on. Imagine, now, that each word can light up. Hence, if you anticipate a verb, say, or an adjective, all words in that particular *column* will light up; also, if you see that the word begins with a particular letter then all the words in that particular *row* will light up. So, what happens if we read a sentence such as

She gave the carrot to the hungry do

If you look at the diagram in Figure 1 you will be able to appreciate what happens when two such cues are combined: all the words in row 'd' light up and so do all the words in the 'noun' column. But any words that are nouns *and* begin with 'd' get twice as much current so they are twice as bright. That's an enormous reduction in the number of possibilities.

Now, suppose we add another kind of cue — number of letters, for example

She gave the carrot to the hungry d_______.

To show how this works we should need three dimensions, not two, i.e., a box, with all the words in each cell spread out according to length along a third dimension.

Figure 2.

Then, if we add a fourth clue, and consider meaning (a fourth dimension), we can see that the remaining possibilities are extremely limited in number — how many hungry six letter things do you know which might get a carrot from a 'she'? (Pollock, 1964). At this point, a glance at almost any of the letters in the focus word would be sufficient for us to decide what the word is. The final letter is, of course, particularly important (Wilson, 1964).

Naturally, the brain itself does not function like this very simple illuminated box. The analogy does, however, provide a useful illustration of the way in which sequences and probabilities affect the brain's performance. In teaching reading we don't need to know how the brain actually does all of this: we don't need to know how the eye works in order to be able to see. On the other hand, we do need to have a good 'feel' for what a child may be doing as s/he strives to recognize words and their meanings; so let us look again at word recognition and the comprehension of word meanings:

1 *Word Recognition*

(a) wE OBviousLY ReLY HeaVily oN oUR KNowledge OF *lETTer SeQUeNces*, ratHER tHaN relyING SOLELY on *wHOle WoRd sHApes*.

(b) We must also rely on our knowledge of probougble *sound sequences* and the *normal pronunciation of any words we enthichipate* — not simply on phonic 'rules'.

2 *Word Comprehension*

We get the meaning of each word from the context in which it appears — not just by looking it up in some mental dictionary once we have 'cracked the code', thus:

(a) Which meaning in this context?

Put it in the bank	Don't bank on it
Climb the bank	Bank to the left

(Most words have more than one possible meaning. Notice how we usually get the intended meaning without a second's thought.)

(b) What meaning from this context?

I grock that is most likely
I love eating nice bloise strawberries

(Notice how easy it is to provide possible meanings for an unfamiliar word in a given context — even an invented 'word' as in these examples.)

Anticipation of sequence and structure, of words and of meanings, is obviously of major importance as a means of recognizing words in normal fluent reading and the role of these 'intermediate skills' must be carefully considered in any plans for developing phonic skills. After all, the vast majority of spelling 'rules' — and their numerous exceptions — are not explicitly taught. Children learn them the way they learn the 'rules' of language — bie beeing ekspozed to them in conteksts wic mak it eezy to cope with unfamiliar wordz and spellingz. We need, therefore, to plan the learning of phonics with this in mind and not deprive children of their seven league boots — opportunities for solving phonic problems by making full use of intermediate skills.

A similar point may be made in relation to some kinds of whole word teaching. Why try to teach by flash cards when a child can get much more benefit from learning how to cope with new words by responding to context? That is how children learnt most of the words they use in everyday speech: that is how you learnt to read, and now read fluently, the vast majority of words you encounter in their varied printed forms.

Most teachers, quite rightly, use a mixture of methods. Consequently, instead of asking the question 'Shall I emphasize whole words of phonics?', we must first ask, 'How can I help children to make better use of context?'

The phonic and whole word issue does not then disappear. It is simply relegated to second place. The important but essentially secondary questions are then:

(i) 'How can I get children to recognize their first few words so that they can provide a context for learning new words?' and
(ii) 'How can I help children to develop an understanding of how letters and spellings work so that they can make more effective use of context in working out unfamiliar spelling patterns independently?'

We need no longer, then, engage in the sterile phonics versus whole-word controversy. Instead, we can get down to a more thoughtful analysis of our own preferred approaches to see how they might be improved in the light of these altered priorities.

Having said this, it is really quite amazing (or is it?) to find that so many parents and teachers have, over the years, come up with a variety of perfectly good answers to all three questions. What their approaches all have in common is the same basic principle that operates when children first learn to talk and in all effective language development thereafter, namely, that language will develop quite naturally when there is a genuine need to communicate.

Children do not learn to talk because parents — or teachers — set out to teach them 'language skills'. They learn to communicate because they want something — a toy, a drink, a pain eased, or attention, and so on.

Children hear the sounds of speech washing round them from the moment of birth. Some of these sounds, or sequences, are repeated time and again and are associated regularly with familiar feelings or events. With quite incredible intellectual facility, children abstract from all of this the rules of language which govern their developing speech — without any formal lessons in phonetics or in grammar.

Similarly in the case of reading, very many parents draw attention to print when print happens to be a useful means of communicating — captions on a child's drawings, brief messages on letters, words on a simple recipe when a child helps a parent to bake a cake, words on shopping lists, labels on goods selected from the shelf at the local supermarket, and so on. These printed forms of language gradually begin to make sense just as spoken language does from an essentially similar process.

As to the intermediate skills, every time a child writes something down for a child's convenience, and pauses for the child to say what comes next, the child is learning about sequence, structure, and anticipation of possible alternatives. Every time a parent pauses in reading an interesting story, the child is motivated to anticipate what comes next. Anticipation at word, phrase and paragraph level is simply a normal part of any interesting act of communication. To the good parent, and the good teacher, there is no need even to think about it — it is just a question of doing what comes naturally! Letter games, sound games, letter-sound games, word games and phrase games may also be used — but for fun, not for instruction.

The damage sets in when we set out to teach from our own agenda instead of taking full advantage of all the potentially interesting experiences that crop up every day which *happen* to involve the need to communicate in speech or in writing. The damage is made worse every time we design drills for skills to be performed whenever we dictate — instead of games that children can return to as and when the spirit moves. It is exacerbated when we incorporate each new analysis of reading skills in ever larger and more complex reading schemes and so-called laboratories and workshops.

No wonder so many children have difficulty in learning to read. Imagine what it would be like if we handed babies over to language laboratory enthusiasts for lessons in talking!

How, then, might we now evaluate cloze procedure (Taylor, 1953) as a means of developing intermediate skills? This now well-known technique consists of presenting texts to children from which words, or parts of words, have been deleted. The children may then be asked either to fill in the gaps, or to discuss the relative virtues of the various possible alternatives they may suggest. Words may be deleted at random, or particular kinds of words may be deleted, for example, all verbs, all adjectives, or words which can only be identified by making some kind of inference or deduction.

Since Rankin (1959) there has been a veritable cascade of publications, including some by the present writer, which have advocated a variety of different strategies for using cloze texts for developing reading skills. As yet, however, there is no clear evidence that would, in my view, justify its use in anything other than a minor support role. Certainly, a good teacher can take almost any strategy and make it work. What is important is that the teacher should choose to use cloze procedure, or any other strategy for skill development, when it provides a means of sharpening a pupil's understanding of something that has arisen in the course of some activity of much greater educational significance.

There are so many natural opportunities for developing intermediate skills that it seems rather a pity to invent artificial strategies. Every time a child reads a difficult text there is an extra opportunity for using intermediate skills. It is much more likely that they will in fact be developed, however, if the child has his or her own good reason for extracting the relevant ideas or information. If two or more children cooperate in struggling with fairly difficult texts, and comparing the information obtained from different texts, that seems likely to provide a much better basis for skill development than working laboriously through sets of exercises whose content is likely to be irrelevant to anything else the child is currently studying. A study of cloze procedure, and its possible uses, therefore, may be of greatest value in helping teachers to see more clearly how to take full advantage of other opportunities that regularly arise without having recourse to cloze procedure!

Concluding Comment

Any adequate analysis of skills must obviously take account of the total context within which those skills are to be exercised. In the case of language and reading skills the context is the child's everyday life experiences. If these are impoverished, the need to communicate is accordingly reduced. Where the communicative purposes for reading and speech are absent, or largely artificial, they become, to that extent, meaningless activities. But reading and reading development depend heavily, as we have already seen, on a response to meaning.

For our starting point, then, in developing any or all of the reading skills we choose to identify, we must of necessity look first at the quality — and range — of *each individual child's* classroom experiences — minute by minute, week by week, and term by term. As we do so, we need to ask ourselves one basic question: 'What does it all add up to?' (Merritt, 1974; Open University, 1980). Perhaps, if we looked much more closely at these educational starting points — and acted accordingly — we should need to spend far less time and energy on the study of reading and development of specific reading skills.

References

CHALL, J.S. (1967) *Learning to Read: The Great Debate*, New York, McGraw-Hill.

HUEY, E.B. (1908) *The Psychology and Pedagogy of Reading*, New York, MacMillan reprinted (1968) Cambridge, MIT Press.

MERRITT, J.E. (1969) 'Reading skills re-examined', *Special Education*, 58, 1.

MERRITT, J.E. (1970) 'The intermediate skills', in GARDNER, K. (Ed.) (1970) *Reading Skills: Theory and Practice*, London, Ward Lock Educational.

MERRITT, J.E. (1974) *What Shall We Teach?* London, Ward Lock Educational.

MILLER, G.A. (1951) *Language and Communication*, New York, McGraw Hill.

OPEN UNIVERSITY (1980) *Curriculum in Action: An Approach to Evaluation*, Open University in association with the Schools Council.

POLLACK, I. (1964) 'Interaction of two sources of verbal context in word identification', *Language and Speech*, 7, pp. 1–12.

RANKIN, E.F. (1959) 'Uses of the cloze procedure in the reading clinic', in FIGUREL, J.A. (Ed.) *Reading in a Changing Society*, Proceedings of the International Reading Association, New York, Scholastic Magazines.

SCHONELL, F.J. (1956) *Backwardness in the Basic Subjects*, Edinburgh, Oliver and Boyd.

TAYLOR, W.L. 'Cloze procedure: A new tool for measuring readability', *Journalism Quarterly*, 30, pp. 415–33.

WILSON, T.W. (1964) *The Effect of Method, Type, Position and Size of Letter Deletion on Syllabic Redundancy in Written English Words*, University of Georgia, dissertation available from University Micro films Inc., 313 North First Street, Ann Arbor, Michigan.

*Literacy is Not Enough**

John Pearce

The 'official' definition of literacy is possessing a reading age of 9.0 or more. This condition is usually measured by using standardized tests of one or both of two abilities: reading aloud, with correct stress, a string of discrete items of vocabulary, and completing in an acceptable fashion a series of incomplete sentences. Primary school teachers seem to be divided about the validity of this procedure. At one level it certainly appears to work. That is, it provides a useful guide to the relative performance of children in tasks which have some close bearing on the ability to read books and texts. At another level it is thought to be unsatisfactory, since there are many instances, in the ordinary class teacher's experience, of children whose actual reading of books and texts appears either much better or much worse than the performance indicated by the tests. I do not propose to enquire further, at this point, into the linguistic validity of reading-age tests. Rather, I want in this article to go on to the next stage, as it were, and look more closely at the phase between achieving literacy and being ready to meet the demands which secondary education places on the linguistic competence of children of 11. I shall draw heavily on insights provided by a number of linguists, but shall try to avoid using the technical language of linguistics. Also, while there is obviously a great deal which could be discussed in the domain of spoken language, I shall here be concerned chiefly with written text.

1

The question to be discussed may be put in this form: what are the features of written text which a child has to learn, or acquire, or become familiar with, in order to meet the demands implicit in the normal secondary curriculum, which are not part of achieving literacy as officially defined? This question has been raised by a number of studies. Barnes

* Originally published in *Cambridge Journal of Education*, 2, 3, 1972.

(1969) in a widely influential paper suggests that secondary education employs a vocabulary and syntax which are distinctive. Several of Bernstein's papers carry the clear message that much of educational failure is linguistic failure, and do so on the basis of contrasts observed in spoken language between different social classes. (There is a good, non-technical account in Chapter 6 of Hannam *et al.* (1971).) Lawton (1968) draws similar conclusions from a study which asked children to write rather than talk. None of these studies, however, has looked at secondary schooling from the rather narrower standpoint involved here. That is, if we inspect written text, and particularly the written texts which form the staple materials of first-year secondary schooling, what differences shall we find from those which form the basis of schooling at the reading-age of 9?

To pursue this question, I propose to make a deliberately simplified contrast between two broad classes of text. On the one hand, most children learn to read by using specially written material. Whatever the approach to initial literacy may be (and no preferences about this are assumed or implied here), the subsequent stage for the vast majority involves a progression through 'readers' which are 'graded'. The nature and validity of this grading, again, are not at issue here. But almost all such reading scheme texts, and a great many readers for primary school use which are modelled on them, are characterized by certain clear features as texts. Their print-size is relatively large, margins are wide, paragraphing is short, illustrations are frequent. The vocabulary is normally subject to quite stringent controls based on word-frequency, and the syntax usually avoids complex structures. (Thus, Beatrix Potter's description of lettuce as 'soporific' is not the only ground on which her tales would not have been published as reading material for infants today.) If you set a representative sample of middle-junior reading books side by side with a representative sample of first-year secondary textbooks, you will find an immediate and striking contrast. The text of the latter is physically much more full and dense — there is much more print to the page. Lines and paragraphs are longer, the controls on vocabulary are less obvious (if present at all), and those on syntax appear at a cursory glance to be much more uneven. The contrast between these two broad classes of written text, which is confessedly very rough and ready, I propose to use as a basis for looking more closely at the precise differences between them. For convenience, they will be referred to respectively as Scheme Text (or ST) and Running Text (RT).

If there is any substance in these differences, and if they are such as not to permit of explicit instruction, we should be able to identify a number of things which children are presumed to have learned by the time they go to secondary school, but which are not necessarily acquired by becoming literate in the narrow sense. Further, if the features of RT to be outlined are in fact learned by large numbers of children without benefit of explicit instruction, we may gain some insight into the processes of learning as they operate in the native-language field. It does not necessarily follow that the features of written text acquired by children who can read RT with ease will form a set of items for classroom instruction in the junior or the secondary school.

2

On the basis of this provisional distinction between ST and RT, we can identify differences between them which are of four broad kinds. The first, and most obvious, are orthographic in the broad sense. The second kind concerns structure within the sentence. A third has to do with the relationships between sentences, in which the interaction between written text and spoken language may play a significant part. The fourth concerns the pattern of relationships between writer, reader, and content.

The orthographic contrasts between ST and RT are readily dealt with, albeit at the cost of appearing to overstate the difference between the two kinds. In practice we encounter not so much a contrast as a continuum, and space allows us to do no more than characterize the two ends. At the most elementary level, the wordspace itself is more conventionalized in RT than in ST: a space of one 'em' (to use the printer's term) is the norm, and spaces of two ems or three ems will usually be reserved for particular purposes. Again, the spacing of text may quite deliberately serve a writer's purpose in ways which the reader is simply assumed to be able to understand. The same principle holds, but to a greater degree because the contrasts are more often exploited, for the use of upper and lower case, for the use of bold face, *italics*, underlining, changes of typeface or type-size, headings and sub-headings, section-numberings, and so on. In the layout of textbooks, to cite one example, the contrast between Roman and Arabic in such cases as 'II,5' or in 'I (b) 4', is a necessary part of the writer's apparatus, but nothing in normal English work will of itself prepare children for it. Other parts of their school work may do this, of course, but not necessarily, or more than incidentally.

Again obvious, but characteristic of RT and generally absent from ST, is the conventional, differentiated pattern of punctuation. Upper-junior pupils in practice encounter the semi-colon and the colon, as well as the dash and numerous other devices, in their own reference and information reading. So completely do writers of English textbooks and workbooks take this for granted, that when they come to deal with these aspects of punctuation they make a possibly curious assumption about the objectives involved. They assume that their task is to teach children how to *use* such items, presupposing that they already know how to interpret them.

Another contrast between ST and RT has to do with the use of vertical and horizontal space. The word-space has been referred to, but the paragraph indent is another horizontal one which is far from standard, and secondary textbooks frequently use different widths of indentation to denote relationships between paragraphs. Of the vertical spaces, Running Text uses standard chapter-heading spaces and paragraph spaces, but in many examples of Scheme Text these are layout features in the domain of the designer rather than the writer or printer. To extend this aspect of layout upwards for a moment, I would not suppose I am alone in having had sixth-form students who had not yet discovered that many textbooks indicate relationships between paragraphs and sections by varying the width of the margins employed.

Turning to structures within the sentence, it is not necessary to do more than refer in passing to word-order. Most writers and publishers for young children so routinely avoid simple inversion as to present no problem until children meet it in novels and can handle it by matching it to speech. Beyond simple word-order, however, there are less easily perceived sources of difficulty which are usually kept out of ST through the intuition of writer or editor. I propose to illustrate some of these in sentences which are themselves examples of the point being made. Long sentences which place significant subordinate clauses between the subject and the verb tend to be sifted out on stylistic grounds. But if a writer places his subordinate clauses at the beginning, and if he can invoke the technical requirements of his subject-matter to justify this, and if his editor does not stand out for simplification, the poor pupil may face written text which defeats him before he can finish the sentence.

The previous sentence illustrates the 'storage' problem of reading a complex written text, which is analogous in many ways (but not all) to the Short Term Memory of experimental psychology. Strains on the reader's ability to store in this way can derive from a wide variety of acceptable sentence structures. Here is an example of the point, which also, as before, furthers the argument. When a human being is engaged in reading a written text, the mechanism of the brain has to process a visual input, has to retain these items for long enough to enable them to form a pattern, and has to be able if necessary to retrieve them in order to adjust the pattern in the light of new, modifying input. This example uses a single subject to hold together a sequence of clauses. In many kinds of RT this type of structure will be broken down into component sentences, but as we shall see in a moment this may not entirely meet the case.

The point to be made here is that writers do not wilfully use structures which are more complex than those of the spoken language. Rather, sentences which use the syntax of the language in this way (though not to the same degree of obscurity) can be found in plenty of secondary school textbooks because they are *written*. That is, the writer can assume them to be open to reinspection (Joos, 1962). And here we meet a very difficult problem: how is a child to know, or indeed *is* he to know, when a text he encounters has been written on the assumption that getting the meaning out of it may call for several readings of it? We all know that we can do things with speech that writing cannot do. It is less widely appreciated that the reinspection that writing is capable of enables it to do things that speech cannot do. But writing can do this effectively only if the reader is party to the contract, so to speak. (One of the problems of secondary English teaching is that a habitual reinspection of text for meaning is not necessarily produced by sustained practice, in English lessons, in reinspecting written text for value.) Writers habitually exploit the capacity of written text for bearing layers of meaning, qualifications and provisos, and if they were always conscious of doing so they might not be so successful in conveying their messages.

(One particular aspect of written text, of the formal, to-be-reinspected sort, which contrasts increasingly with text written for young children, is its avoidance of the informalities usually associated with speech. The dialogue printed in many scheme readers is frequently life-like, or attempts to be so. Textbooks, however, have to go out of their way to avoid falling foul of the folk-linguistic notions (cf. Doughty *et al.*, 1972) of teachers. To take a current example of such notions, the usage 'hopefully' is restricted in RT to 'with hope', but in ST it may have the now common spoken-language meaning of 'One hopes that'. This particular change is now giving us *undoubtably*, has already given us *regrettably*, *happily*, and much else — and will in due time give us *forgettably*, *pitiably*, and many more 'protestables'.)

This is only a selection of the syntactic contrasts which can be found between ST and RT, and each reader may care to look at textbooks in his own subjects to see how far they unwittingly present problems of reading to the children for whom they are intended. I have not cited any here because it would not be fair to cite only a very few, and I have not space to cite more.

3

A third category of contrasts between ST and RT concerns the relationships between sentences. This aspect of text, known in linguistics as discourse analysis, is relatively much less fully explored than the grammar of the sentence. Educationally it is an area of critical importance for it refers, among other things, to those features of a text which make it possible to follow who is who in a narrative, to follow what happens when, and to follow or infer what happens for what reasons and with what results. In the case of identifying who is who, the reader needs to be able to identify the participants although each participant may be given a wide variety of labels. In following the time-sequence, the clues given in the tense-system may be vital. Inferring cause and effect will require the accurate and immediate interpretation of items such as *hence*, *so*, *and so*, *since*, *because*, *so that* — and in English there may be six or more meanings, at this level of interpretation, to both *and* and *but*. The reader who cares to pursue this topic in detail can refer to Hasan (1969) and Hasan and Halliday (forthcoming). Here it will be simpler to illustrate by using an example given in another context by Gleason (1968). The example is American, but the British reader will readily translate it.

> A tall, lanky high-school basketball star folded himself into the little foreign car with his short, pudgy father beside him. The son drove carefully down the busy highway, obviously restrained by the older man's presence. He watched the other traffic intently. He signalled before each turn and came to a full stop at the blinker. Classmates stared in amazement, but the driver took no notice of them. The athlete's strange behaviour seemed totally inexplicable. The poor boy was obviously in some trouble.

Gleason's commentary reads: 'This passage has been contrived to include a range of phenomena . . . and to give some of them slight exaggeration. There are two participants. On introduction each is given a certain amount of description. Aside from whatever literary function such description may have, it serves also to define initially the set of contrasts which will be used, from place to place, to identify these participants. For example, one is described as a *basketball star*; toward the end of the paragraph he can, therefore, be identified by *athlete*. It is not the description, as such, that counts, but the contrasts that are set up. For example, *the son* serves as an identification in the second sentence because the other participant has been described as *father*, and in a somewhat more complex manner *older man* exploits the same contrast . . . Subsequent identifications use selections of the available features and so take on much of the aspect of paraphrase. Not only so, the corpus of usable identifications is cumulative. Thus, the action 'drive' in the second sentence is added in such a way that *driver* becomes a possible label several sentences later.' Gleason goes on to point out that in English pronouns have a special place in this system of participant-identification; these are dealt with in some detail by Hasan (1968), from a somewhat different point of view.

What is implied here is not that children of 11 should be taught to respond to these and other, analogously important aspects of written text, but that a great deal of the writing they will encounter assumes that they can so respond. Moreover, a good proportion of children internalise these features of written text successfully, yet no English teacher would ever try to instruct his pupils in them. The implication must be that many children who are 'literate' may have a great deal of learning to do about the nature of written text, but that on the whole they can do this without explicit instruction, if the context for it can be successfully created. (This means nothing more ominous than persuading as many children as possible to read as many substantial books as possible — but there can be more than one idea of what may be possible.)

It was suggested above that in the matter of the relations between sentences the bearing of spoken language might be important. In the complete absence of research it is probably too simple to suppose that the person who is good at reading aloud is also likely to be a good silent reader. This may be true, but plenty of good silent readers do not read aloud well. At the same time, the textual features such as pronouns, participant identifiers, concords of tense, and the like which serve to give a text its continuousness (which Hasan and Halliday call *cohesion ties*) have their analogies in the spoken language. Continuous spoken discourse often makes very careful use of intonational features, such as the segmenting of discourse into tone-groups, parallelism in the placing of stress, or echo in the choice of pitch-changes. The educational problem is that while most native speakers are intuitively aware of intonation as a matter of making choices among many available patterns, they have to learn, or discover, that a written text may be ambiguous in meaning until its spoken equivalent can be selected. Many secondary children are apt to suppose, in reading a scripted play for example, that the lines to be read aloud have, in each case, only one 'right' version in speech. The trials of the Schools Council Language in Use Project revealed that looking at the many ways in which one particular set of words can be uttered can help a class to realise that reading a text aloud is, among other things, a matter of choosing the intonation patterns to apply — and these have to derive from their prior knowledge of the spoken language. (Doughty *et al.*, 1971.)

The fourth category of contrasts between ST and RT need not detain us long. Consider the last sentence in the quotation from Gleason's invented text (above): 'the poor boy was obviously in some trouble'. There is a clear inference suggested by *obviously* about the perceptions of the spectators, but in *the poor boy* there is an attitude expressed to which the reader is expected to respond. Now, if a linguist can bring this about when we know he is conning us, the ability of a novelist to bring it about not once but many times with an audience of children is likely to be considerable. Linguistically what is being modified here is the relationships in the triangle formed by the writer, his subject-matter, and the reader. The writer may seek both to modify the reader's response to the content and to change his interpretation of the writer's view of it. But these two possibilities are independent of one another, and no very great literary skill is required to modify a reader's view of content without alerting him to, or while concealing from him, any change in the writer's view.

The notion that writers of children's books, fiction or non-fiction, do not have attitudes to their subject-matter, or do not try to affect their readers' responses to it in any way, I take to be self-evidently naïve. But whereas the RT of history textbooks uses a wide range of items which allow the writer to convey his attitudes to subject-matter very clearly (in particular the comment-adjuncts, such as *unfortunately*, *at last*, *wisely*), this resource is nothing like so fully available to the writer of ST because the vocabulary permitted does not include many of them. This has the curious effect of making the attitudes of writers of ST not less evident to the reader, but more. And there is a long tradition of approval of this situation in the literature of fairy story. Somewhere, somehow, children have to learn or discover the less perceptible ways in which writers convey their attitudes to content. As secondary schooling progresses, too, the serious scholar also has to discover how writers express the more subtle attitudes themselves — those of qualification and tentativeness. It is a reasonable supposition that the sixth-former who can express these attitudes in his own writing has been able to respond to them in his reading for a considerable period. It would be interesting to know for how long, because the sixth-former who cannot express himself in this way is likely to be studying science or to be heading for disaster in his examinations, and even science is stepping up its demands on this kind of linguistic competence in the student.

4

Underlying my catalogue of the features of written language typical of secondary schooling run two questions with much wider implications. One is the question whether this catalogue ought not to become, at some suitable stage of schooling, a programme of instruction of children, and if not, why not. The other is the question whether I am not claiming for the written language a status, a degree of independence of the spoken language and a degree of distinctiveness, which the facts do not warrant.

The short answer to the first question is, surely, that it is not in the nature of language to be susceptible of that kind of treatment. Compared with our success in enabling our own infants to learn their native language, our failure in teaching older children a second one is not encouraging. Further, the objective of the learning is not the conscious knowledge of a set of identifiable and retrievable items, but the internalized knowledge in which consciousness plays a minimal part. In other words, if teachers of upper juniors resolve that every one of their pupils shall be persuaded to read a Puffin book once a fortnight, they will rightly focus the interest and attention of the child on the story, but will do this the more confidently because they also know what the reading is doing in other respects. They know, that is to say, that such sustained exposure to RT is enabling the children to internalize a great many of the items in my catalogue, and quite painlessly into the bargain. This is why in this article I have used the word 'learn' with some hesitation, often with a gloss like 'or discover'.

The one possible exception to this rule may be sentence structure, especially for the child of below-average ability. Fraser's attempt to programme the learning of syntactic options (Fraser, 1969 f.) has some fascinating aspects, but here again the emphasis is in teaching the child to perform expressively, when what may be at issue is the child's lack of experience in the reception aspect of written language.

The second question is not so easily answered. Partly it is a matter of how we look at the problem: if we are unaccustomed to so studied a contrast between spoken and written language, we shall suspect that the contrast is over-drawn. Partly, too, contrasts have a habit of getting over-drawn when one is trying to draw them. On the other hand, most grammar-school teachers have experienced the very gifted student on paper who could not talk in an academic setting at all, just as most other kinds of teacher have met the very gifted talker whose mastery of written language, whether as reader or as writer, was defective or worse. In either case the pupil so one-sided is the product of emphases in his education, and confirms Barnes' suggestion that the language that children learn in school is a combination of what they are taught and what the school teaches unwittingly. And the centrality of written language, not merely in the secondary school, not even in higher education, but in basic employ-ability in the latter part of this century, needs no arguing here. One might argue that if most educational failure is linguistic failure, *tout court*, then much educational under-achievement is failure in handling written language.

The advocates of context-support methods in the teaching of initial literacy (for example, Morris, 1965) postulate a continuous line of development which goes on into the secondary school. But after formal literacy has been achieved children are supposed by many teachers to find adequate contexts for their reading in their search for information. This has practical effect in the equipping of primary school library stocks with large quantities of informational reading. I would argue that for many children far more potent and supportive contexts lie in the child's engagement in a story, and this would have the practical effect of even larger quantities of children's fiction in the school. I could wish that the paperback revolution had happened in every school, and that every teacher was aware of the riches in his grasp.

References

BARNES, D., (1969) *Language, The Learner, and The School*, Penguin.

DOUGHTY, P., PEARCE, J., and THORNTON, G.M., (1971) *Language in Use*, Arnold, (Especially cf. Unit C6.)

DOUGHTY, P., PEARCE, J., and THORNTON, G.M. (1972) *Exploring Language*, Arnold.

FRASER, A., (1969) *Control and Create*, Heinemann.

GLEASON, H.A., JR., (1968) 'Contrastive analysis in discourse structure', in ALATIS, J.E. (Ed.), *19th Annual Round Table Linguistics Series*, Georgetown U.P.

HANNAM, C., SMYTH, P., and STEPHENSON, N., (1971) *Young Teachers and Reluctant Learners*, Penguin.

HASAN, R., (1969) *Grammatical Cohesion in Spoken and Written English, Pt. I*, Longman.

HASAN, R., and HALLIDAY, M.A.K., *Grammatical Cohesion in Spoken and Written English, Pt. II*, Longman, forthcoming.

JOOS, M., (1962) *The Five Clocks*, Harcourt Brace.

LAWTON, D., (1968) *Social Class, Language, and Education*, Routledge.

Reading: Effective Communication Through Text

Geoffrey E. Lewis

Introduction

This article sees reading as the act of effective communication through text, implying motivation and ability in both reader and writer. It examines some of the principles of effective communication, relates them to language form, and suggests a process model of reading, which seems most consistent with these two factors, and with current psychological theory.

The implications of this view of reading are considered particularly those concerning the role of the text, the role of the reader and the role of the teacher.

Rationale

Theory and practice of the teaching of early reading are well-developed and exhaustive at or below word level. It is significant that two major pedagogical reading strategies — word recognition and word building — operate at these levels. However, how words work in the context of phrases, sentences and larger text units is not made explicit. It cannot be assumed that meaning is additive; text can be read a word at a time, and its meaning somehow accumulate. The 'meaning' of any text unit can be greater or lesser than the sum of its parts, or in some cases, different. Three constructed sentences illustrate this:

(a) John has arrived
(b) The weather is hot.
(c) Can you shut the door?

In (a) the sentence may have a far greater significance or meaning if it is in a context in which John is the returning prodigal son. In (b) the potential richness of association concerning the word 'weather' is not utilized, and the sentence would appear to be mundane. However such an interpretation must alter if it is considered in a context where people are discussing the likelihood of forest fires. Example (c) has a different meaning from the apparent sum of its parts in that, although apparently a question, most English speakers would interpret it as a polite request or order.

In each case, a more precise meaning is only obtained when the sentence (or whatever unit is considered) is placed in a context. There is, as yet, no satisfactory answer to the problem of what constitutes the 'meaning' of a text (see van Dijk, 1977, for an approach based on the propositional content of any text). However, it would seem that any view of the 'meaning' of a text, must reflect the fact that text production and reading are a form of communication. Therefore, a more comprehensive account of meaning is only approachable when one considers the motivation behind a text being written, and the motivation behind a text being read.

In the teaching of reading 'use of context' is a much-used phrase and it is widely accepted that words are often read more easily (or quicker) when they are 'in context'. Even so, the definition of 'context', and how it facilitates reading is by no means, straightforward. It is useful to distinguish 'context' and 'co-text'. De Beaugrande (1980) writes: 'A text must be relevant to a SITUATION OF OCCURRENCE, in which a constellation of STRATEGIES, EXPECTATIONS and KNOWLEDGE is active. This wide environment can be called CONTEXT; the internal structuring of the text constitutes the CO-TEXT'.

It is clear that we need:

(i) An account of the reading process which can at least suggest how context and co-text work.
(ii) A method of analyzing context and co-text so that structure and process can be integrated.

These areas are discussed in the following three sections of the article. The final section discusses some of the implications of the account provided.

The Reading Process

The Value of Process Models

We have seen how much teaching of reading uses processes which cannot by themselves account for the entire act of reading. One way in which we can improve this state of affairs is to produce a model of the reading process. Such a process model must specify three aspects:

(a) The phenomenon

It is necessary to define the process so that others may judge the validity of the definition. It may seem unnecessary to define 'reading', but in fact the word is ambiguous in a way which can be very misleading. It is a word widely used, and is so common that it is frequently used without reflection, on the assumption that it means the same for everyone at all times. One difficulty is that it has, in fact, a variety of dictionary definitions, each with a different nuance. A greater difficulty is that it is an apparently simple term for what is undoubtedly an extremely complex and not fully understood process. People differ as to how they conceive the process, and such individual conceptions are likely to be unanalyzed and not amenable to objective comment or comparison.

The definition of process is also necessary in order to assess the explanatory power of the rest of the model. If reading is defined as 'effective communication through text', then the model must show how this occurs. If it fails to do so, the model is incomplete, incorrect, or both of these.

(b) The elements

The elements of a model are those parts of sub-skills which in some way work together.

(c) The processes

The processes of a model are the ways in which the elements are sequenced, or interact to produce the phenomenon. Some models envisage a much greater variety of elements and interaction than others, yet any model must still be capable of explaining the wealth of evidence concerning reading at or below word level.

The qualities and features of reading process models are discussed in de Beaugrande (1981). For a useful summary of competing models, see de Beaugrande (1981) and Downing and Leong (1981).

I now propose to discuss the constraints upon model production which are a consequence of the view of reading outlined so far. One particular type of model seems most convincing and comprehensive. A number of interactive reading models have been devised (for example, Rumelhart, 1977; and Woods, 1980) which vary in some of their detail. However, there is sufficient commonality for it to be possible to use the overall concept as an adequate definition for useful consideration with regard to the learning and teaching of reading.

Interactive Reading Models

One of the important facts to be integrated into a process model of reading is the fact that 'context' and/or 'co-text' facilitates reading at word level. It is not sufficient to have a model which works only from small units to larger.

There must be some way in which larger units influence the processing of smaller ones. The reading process is therefore a two-way process. In computer terminology, processes which proceed from small to large units are called Bottom-Up, while those which work from large to small are Top-Down (for example, de Beaugrande, 1981).

The presence of a Top-Down element in reading has important implications, many of which are relevant to the Text Analysis section.

Firstly, there is the question of the nature of units larger than the word. A phrase will certainly have 'meaning' in the sense that it identifies an aspect of the message. A clause will have a complete propositional meaning. Viewed in that way, a sentence may have no more propositional value than a clause. However, in its structure and its relationship to other sentences, it reflects decisions made by the writer at the planning or organizational level. Sentences combine in ways which are not random (see Hoey, 1983) and their organization is determined by the global or higher meaning of the text. Syntax is not the highest level of organization: we also need an account at discourse level.

Secondly, if context facilitates reading at the word level, then any other of the nested levels may be aided by some wider contextual unit.

Thirdly, if context works by making it unnecessary to process all aspects of print before reaching a decision (or 'reading' it), then reading is not necessarily painstakingly exhaustive but may involve partial processing, risk-taking, and the integration of skills rather than the pursuit of a skill to the bitter end.

Fourthly, if context works by suggesting which features of print not yet read will be more productive, then prediction becomes a basic skill, not a higher level skill. The third and fourth points are important and worth reiterating. Context may work not only by reducing the processing load, but also by controlling the nature of such processing.

Fifthly, text units larger than the word have meaning in a way that letters and some words in isolation, do not. If such units of meaning aid the reading process then comprehension must be an on-going process and not an end product, or a higher level skill.

Sixthly, if we assume that comprehension is not necessarily achieved in precisely the same way by each reader and that the nature of such comprehension is not identical for all, then reading will be a different process or balance of processes for each individual reader.

Combining these six factors, our Interactive Reading Model can be summarized as follows.

Information regarding text can be acquired at any of several levels. These levels are organised according to principles which vary from level to level as in Figure 1.

Figure 1.

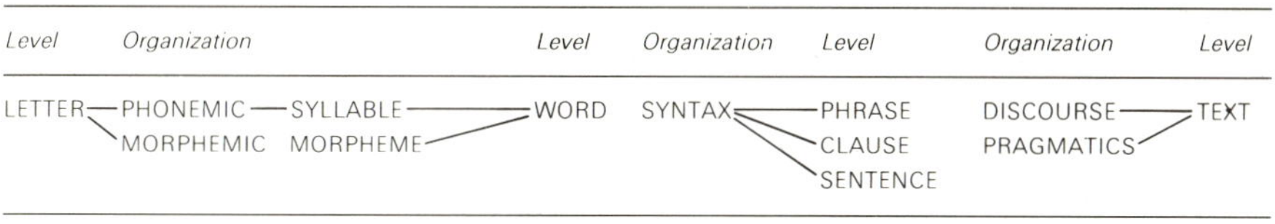

According to the Rumelhart model, reading proceeds in two directions simultaneously — Top/Down and Bottom/Up. Top/Down processing may reduce the amount of Bottom/Up processing, or may even determine its course. Bottom/Up processing will construct units of increasing size.

There is no reason why units only have contact with their neighbour in the nesting hierarchy. It appears that any level may *interact* with any other, in any direction, in the pursuit of reading.

Since we are not consciously aware of all these interactions, most of the processing must be unconscious.

The top levels of organization, namely, discourse and pragmatics, need to be defined and distinguished. Discourse factors refer to the purposeful way in which words and sentences are organized and sequenced in order to fulfil a particular function.

Pragmatics is taken to refer to all aspects of a communicative situation which are not linguistic. Many pragmatic features of oral communication (such as non-verbal gestures, and the ability of the participants to ask each other immediately answerable questions) are not available to those who use the written mode. Some pragmatic features are more typical of written text. Illustrations may be useful in understanding text or reducing the amount of information which needs to be transmitted in written form (for example, Schallert, 1980).

Text Analysis

The process model has suggested those features of text which are relevant to the reading process and which need to be analyzed. In particular, text structures which are concerned with the organization and utilization of information seem particularly important. Structures at or below word level are already well described and are not considered here, except where significant at a higher level of organization. In passing, it is significant that word structure seems better accountable in terms of a *combined* phonemic/morphemic approach than by using either system by itself. This has significance for both word-building and word recognition activities (for example, Glushko, 1981).

The higher levels of text organization principles can be described in terms of *motivation* and *manifestation*. Surface form is a manifestation of some motive and each motive has its repertoire of possible manifestations. Successful reading involves making the link from one to the other.

Syntax

Syntax comprises a set of formalized rules, often considered merely in terms of grammaticality and acceptability. However, it is useful to consider syntax not as a system by itself, but as a system in interaction with others. For example, in considering the relationship between syntax and semantics, two complementary relationships are apparent. The 'semantics of syntax' is concerned with the meaning(s) of any syntactic form, while the 'syntax of semantics' is concerned with the possible syntactic realization(s) of semantic content. One important implication of this viewpoint is that while a relatively complete set of syntactic rules may be available at an early age, the matching of such rules to semantic content may need a lifetime to develop. While syntax comprises a set of rules, the *use* of syntax reflects the discourse constraints in operation (Reid, 1983; and Perera, 1982).

Discourse Factors — Content

It is axiomatic that since text often reflects complex situations, then difficult, complex or novel topics will tend to produce difficult text. Beyond being aware of the fact, this point is of little use in text analysis, because one cannot often simplify or change the real world. However, one way of examining the content of text is to analyze the *nature* of the information which it hopes to communicate.

Green and Morgan (1981) suggest that text may represent a number of different kinds of meaning. It is the readers' task to determine the nature of the meaning(s) of any text unit. In illustration Green and Morgan use the sentence 'He is allergic to chocolate'.

In the illustration, the *propositional meaning* is that a masculine subject, known or referred to, is allergic to chocolate.

But it is the case that, in the illustrative sentence, the propositional analysis does not tell us who is allergic to chocolate. However, the use of the word 'he' suggests that fuller information is available, either from the co-text or the immediate environment. This is the *linguistic meaning* of the sentence. There is also the *speech act meaning*.

Austin (1962) and Searle (1969) observe that any utterance involves three 'acts'. The locutionary act is that of producing the words to be heard or read. The illocutionary act is a social act, which concerns the purpose or motivation behind the utterance. In different contexts, the illustrative sentence could perform such illocutionary acts as statement, denial, or contradiction. The third type of act, the perlocutionary act, is concerned with the actual effect, planned or unplanned, of the utterance. Again, in different contexts, the effect of saying 'He is allergic to chocolate' may be to induce sympathy, disappointment, concern, etc.

Together with speech act meaning there is *implicational meaning* which is dependent upon context. For instance, the implication of saying 'He is allergic to chocolate' is different if one considers it as a response to the following two utterances:

(a) 'Can I give your child a piece of chocolate?'
(b) 'Your child has just eaten a piece of chocolate'.

Thus the task of identifying meaning in a text may represent different demands on the reader, who will need the ability to perceive the types of meaning as they are represented in the text being read.

Interpersonal Discourse Factors

The discussion on types of meaning makes it clear that surface form is only a starting point in the process of understanding or interpretation. In addition, the dialogues used above are only coherent if one assumes that the 'child' and 'he' refer to the same person. Grice (1975) suggests a number of maxims which operate to make conversation coherent. Grice does not give the maxims the status of 'laws' which cannot be broken. Each is seen as a normal procedure, which may be broken. However, if this happens the utterance becomes marked, and the flouting has a communicative significance.

His maxims are:

(i) Cooperation

It is reasonable to assume that both parties are *cooperating* to try to achieve a mutually satisfactory communication. If either party perceives that the other is uncooperative, a very different strategy is required. In narrative text, this can be important as any character and even the narrator, may be trying to mislead the reader.

(ii) Quantity

'. . . make your contribution as informative (but not more informative than) is required'. At first, it may seem odd to be critical of extra information. However, such is communicative motivation that the hearer/reader will seek to integrate all mentioned items, and the extra *quantity* of information may therefore be misleading or overload the processing capacity.

(iii) Quality

'... do not say what you believe to be false, or that for which you lack adequate evidence'. In certain text types, for instance, narrative or propaganda, this principle is knowingly violated with valid reason (as in the creation of suspense in a story).

(iv) Relation

This maxim concerns the need to be relevant. Relevance is not always apparent, if one considers only adjacent sentences. For instance, in a detective story, a clue may not reveal its relevance until the last page. Irrelevant material will produce the same problem for the reader as content which breaks the Quantity maxim.

(v) Manner

This maxim includes such features as 'be orderly' and 'avoid ambiguity' — surely hallmarks of effective discourse.

It is possible to argue that the maxims Grice saw as governing conversation as a co-operative act, equally apply to written text. They have value as a series of frames, through which text can be viewed in order to determine the way in which the writer guides the reader through the text.

General Psychological Discourse Factors

Texts are written to be processed, and textual features which have a direct bearing on human processing are best described as conventions or default assumptions. Such conventions can be disregarded or broken, often to great effect, but when this happens there is frequently a definite communicative reason (if the text is well-written, as opposed to inept or bizarre). The norm creates pattern which emphasizes the effect created when the conventions are broken.

The conventions are:

(i) Topic-Comment (Theme-Rheme)

In simplified terms the topic or theme is equivalent to 'what I am going to talk about', and the comment, or rheme, comprises 'what I am going to say about it.' Communication is normally most effective, therefore, if the Topic precedes the Comment. In a simple declarative sentence such as 'John broke the window'; 'John' is the topic and the remainder comprises the comment. It is possible to analyze each clause or sentence in this way but it is important to realize that the convention may be broken for reasons suggested in following sections. In any case, the selection of a 'topic' for any particular sentence is often only explicable in terms of the wider discourse. Sentence and Discourse topics may not coincide, and the relationship between them is as important as either by itself.

(ii) Given-New

It is communicatively efficient to open a text unit with something which is known or given, and then to add new information relating to it. The simple dichotomy suggested by the terms Given and New fail to reflect the fact it is difficult to thoroughly define either. Dahl (1976) suggests four types of distinguishable 'Given' information:

(a) Previously mentioned (in the same text)
(b) Known v. not known (in term of world knowledge)
(c) Activated v. non activated (activation may be indirect)
(d) Predictable v. unpredictable.

Only one of these, (a), can be definitively described by analysis of the text alone. This reinforces the observation that any text analysis must be incomplete if it is considered in isolation from any reader.

The combination of Topic-Comment form and Given-New structure is revealed in three common text patterns. Such thematic progressions can be described as follows:

(a) Simple Linear T.P.

$T_1 \quad C_1$

$\qquad T_2\ (= C_1) \quad C_2$

'The giant frightened everybody'
'They hid in the wood'

(b) T.P. with Continuous Theme

$T_1 \quad C_1$

$\qquad T_2\ (= T_1) \quad C_2$

'The giant frightened everybody'
'He ran after them'

(c) T.P. with Derived Theme

$\qquad\qquad T$

$T_1 \quad C_1$

$\qquad\qquad\qquad T_2 \quad C_2$

'The giant was huge'
'His hand was enormous'
'His feet were like bathtubs'

In an important paper, Daneš (1974) shows how sentences can be effectively described, not in syntactic terms, but in terms of their information structure.

(iii) Fore-grounding-backgrounding

Items which are important in the message (at that point in the communication) will tend to be fore-grounded, while less-important items will be back-grounded. This can be done in a variety of ways. For instance:

(a) Repetition. An oft-repeated item will have high salience.

(b) Recency. A newly-mentioned item will be fore-grounded, and will tend to recede, if not mentioned again.
(c) Sentence position. A sentence, with its initial capital letter, full stop, and spacing, forms a perceptual unit. Items at either end of the sentence tend to have greater salience than those in the middle.
(d) Communicative importance. Importance of any text item is related not only to its innate qualities, but also to its function within the message to be communicated. Perception of this by the reader will depend upon knowledge of the world and importantly, knowledge of the purpose of the text.

(iv) Clarity

Text is said to have greater clarity if there is a one-to-one relation between the words and their referent. For example, 'the toy is broken' would be said to have greater clarity than 'the toy's broken', although a fluent hearer/reader may not notice the difference. In the above instance, clarity is reduced by combining two morphemes (toy/is) into one perceptual unit. The motivation for such a reduction is discussed below. For further discussion, see Bates and MacWhinney (1979).

(v) Rapidity

Other things being equal, text processing is more efficient if rapid. This constraint often runs contrary to other factors (for instance, the example 'the toy's broken'). In some cases, whole chunks may be omitted, in the assumption that the reader will fill in, by means of logic or by the activation of an appropriate schema or plan. Some estimates suggest that the proportion of stated: unstated information in narrative is 1:8 (Graesser, 1981).

(iv) Overlap of features i–v

It often happens that a particular surface form is a manifestation of more than one of the above features. For instance, the initial sentence element is commonly the topic, is commonly given, and is commonly the subject of the sentence. This can be called the default assumption. Any deviation from this is often significant and, in some way 'marks' an element of the message. Such marking is only effective if the default is commonly perceived.

Text represents a state of tension. If default assumptions, as defined in the previous sections, were always observed the resulting text(s) would be rather dull and unexciting. The writer's task is to create an effect by selectively breaking such 'rules', while ensuring that the text continues to cohere.

Pragmatic Factors

Pragmatic Factors Within the Reader

It is clear that for successful reading to take place, a reader has to possess far more in the way of skills than is suggested in most skill inventories or readiness profiles. We have already seen how some texts are only comprehensible if the reader can appreciate the type of knowledge being communicated can infer implicit content, and can apprehend (even unconsciously) communicative devices and intentions.

It is impossible to attempt an exhaustive list of 'reader qualities' which are necessary if successful reading is to occur. The impossibility arises from the fact that any human capacity or skill may be needed at some time in the business of text interpretation. Any attempt to produce such a list is also potentially misleading because any finite list may close the mind to other, unmentioned factors. De Beaugrande (1980, pp. 278–9) suggests a list of twenty-one abilities necessary for effective text processing.

Here is a sample to illustrate how the concept of 'basic skills' can be enhanced and extended:

(a) ability to focus and distribute attention, wisely;
(b) ability to analyze and learn from failure;
(c) reasoning by causality;
(d) reasoning by generalization;
(e) hierarchical reasoning;
(f) analogical reasoning;
(g) reasoning from incomplete knowledge;
(h) self-reliance in intellectual undertakings of all kinds.

Not all these skills are amenable to introspection or abstract manipulation. Children, and indeed successful adult readers intuitively use them with increasing success, in their learning and understanding of spoken language. The critical factor is the opportunity which is provided for children to assess the success or otherwise of their efforts. Since it is a feature of written text, that it does not provide the same feedback as, for instance, conversation, then the provision of adequate feedback for reader becomes an important teaching point.

Pragmatic Factors Within Text

One aspect of text interpretation which has not yet been discussed, is that of text purpose. It is dangerous to try to reduce such a quality to a finite taxonomy. An attempt to do so would have to account for all human motivations in reading and writing, and also has to be cognisant of the fact that any text may serve more than one purpose as a whole or in part, and may be *designed* to have different purposes for different readers.

Some of the difficulties become apparent upon even a rudimentary analysis of the narrative form. It is safe to say that narrative form follows a time line, possibly with use of flashback or forward planning. Many narratives only make sense if an assumption of progress through time is made. It is also safe to observe that narratives largely concern characters and their action, events and consequences. However, the process becomes less sure when we note that stories often do not merely reflect real-life probability. In fact, many real-life probabilities would usually make a boring story. Nevertheless, even young children have a perception of 'storyness' i.e. what will make a good story, as opposed to what is most likely. Stories comprise surprise and suspense, yet in some way these subjective qualities seem to follow some sort of pattern. 'Storyness' and children perception of that quality are discussed in Lewis (1983).

Cohesion is an aspect of the characterization of text which has been exhaustively defined and classified (Halliday and Hasan, 1976). It aims to demonstrate the ways in which a text can be recognized and used as an unified text, rather than a collection of unconnected or random units. However, the role of cohesive factors in the reading process is not clear. Halliday and Hasan claim that for a text to be a text, and therefore comprehensible, it must contain cohesive devices, and that text is recognized as cohesive because of such devices. However, the construction of meaning in this manner (bottom-up) is only one possible process in the interpretation and understanding of text. The danger of any purely linguistic system, such as cohesion, is to regard such features as the means by which understanding is achieved. In terms of process, the assumption must be questioned. The essential question is 'Does the cohesive structure of text cause cohesion, or does it merely reflect the coherent nature of the content?' Certainly cohesive text can be incoherent and text which displays no cohesive device can be made coherent by mean of some gap-filling inference as in the following conversation:

'What time is it?'
'Get on with your work'

In terms of efficient text processing, it seems that world knowledge and expectation on behalf of the reader make a text coherent, even if this involves ignoring or misperceiving surface form (Lewis, 1983). Linguistic structure is used to do a repair job when the reader's understanding breaks down.

The ability to use linguistic structure to *produce* meaning rather than *confirm* meaning is almost certainly developmental in nature. If this is so, it is unreasonable to expect young children to show mastery of the act, and the failure of a child to do so is no more significant than the observation that he is not yet fully grown. For further discussion of the role of cohesion in particular, see Urquhart (1983), Green and Morgan (1981) and de Beaugrande (1980).

Implications for Teachers

The view of reading, as described in this article, has many implications. These will be discussed under four headings:

(i) The curriculum.
(ii) Skilled performance and teaching techniques.
(iii) Materials for reading.
(iv) Diagnosis in reading.

(i) The Curriculum

In the interactive model of reading, comprehension is seen as an ongoing part of the reading process, and therefore the readers' ability to understand the content of the text at any point as it progresses, will affect the nature and possibly the outcome of the process. Since 'text' can cover the whole range of human experiences, it follows that reading will require knowledge and skills that can only be acquired through a broadly-based curriculum. It is difficult to envisage any child, or group of children, for whom this does not apply. Certainly it is important for children of limited ability and for those with reading difficulties. Undue concentration on a narrow set of skills may well have little or even harmful effect. Many of the more narrowly defined reading skills operate at the low-level end of the reading process. As such, they may not be independent or autonomous, in which case the factors which influence such low-level skills also need consideration. Many of the more powerful processes are not easily defined and assessed, but this is no reason to ignore them.

Teaching of low-level skills is often rule-based, as in some phonics teaching. This may be diametrically opposed to the way in which children naturally learn. Spoken language acquisition is best accounted for not by assuming that children learn by applying a set rule to experiential data, but by noting that children form rules by examination of such data in a meaningful context. There is no reason to suppose that reading acquisition does not follow the same pattern.

In terms of curriculum, the child needs to set out from a wide range of experience of the type that will provide the greatest amount of data and feedback for rule acquisition and application. Teachers need professional confidence to argue against a restriction of the curriculum in the pursuit of greater accountability.

(ii) Skilled Performance and Teaching Techniques

We have seen how reading involves a wider range of skills than has been commonly envisaged. Three major points arise from the concept of skilled performance.

Firstly, it is clear that *integration* of skills is just as important as performance of any skill in isolation. Isolated skill practice ignores this point. No single system (for example, phonic rules or syntax) within language leads to efficient reading in itself. Redundancy operates in language not because there is a redundancy within a particular system, such as symbol-sound correspondence, but because it exists across a number of systems. It is only by combining information, and moving from one system or level to another that text can be unravelled. A further danger, in some skill teaching, is the assumption that performance will transfer automatically from one context to another. Yet the context in which a task is performed influences and even dictates the way in which task is accomplished. It is also true that any skill is best learned to the stage of autonomous use, when its relevance to the end point (in this case, reading) can be perceived by the child, who can notice how variation in skill performance affects performance on the objective.

The second point of issue about skilled performance is the nature of the route via which skilled performance is attained. One view appears to be that 100 per cent accuracy is a starting point and skipping, guessing or skimming is only for a higher level of performance. This belief results in criteria such as knowledge of all words before a child reads a book. This need not be the case. We may view 100 per cent accuracy as the end point. The consequent relaxation of the stringent criterion will take a lot of pressure away from the reader. In addition, if all words are known prior to text reading it may be that the reader's ability to perceive and use contextual clues in order to work out discourse meaning is not practised, and its importance not realized.

In any case, 100 per cent accuracy can be misleading. It is possible for children to know all the words, and still not be able to comprehend a passage, owing to semantic, syntactic or pragmatic difficulties.

A second 100 per cent fallacy is that of 100 per cent independence. Children's reading is often judged against this yardstick. Thus, a few 'errors' are permitted, while a few more create the child's 'frustration level'. This takes no notice of the type and importance of the errors, and disregards the child's motivation to read a particular text.

If a distinction is made between reading as evidence of mastery, and reading as part of the learning to read process, then, for the latter, 100 per cent mastery may become irrelevant. In adult-child conversation there are many ways in which the adult can manage the situation, providing instruction, support or feedback as required. It is possible to see parallel activities in reading. For instance, it becomes very reasonable for someone other than the child to do most or all of the reading. The child may contribute as much as he/she wishes, from the odd word to most of the passage. It becomes reasonable to practice a passage as often as is necessary, either the child alone, or the child following someone else's reading. In each case, the child has access both to the printed symbol and to the content. This link is vital, if the young reader is to perceive how one relates to the other.

The third point about skilled performance concerns the question 'performance of what?'. Skilled reading usually involves reading accurately, independently *and* silently. It is important to assess how much of a child's reading is performed aloud, and how much is silent. Reading aloud may impose an extra task, the phonemic realization of the word. It certainly imposes an articulatory task, and it arguably imposes a rigid insistence on left-right reading with no opportunity to suspend judgment on a word. This may well be a reasonable criterion for the demonstration of reading mastery, but is it valid for learning or practice? The reader may well feel that the end-point is word-by-word accuracy rather than understanding appreciation and enjoyment. Many young children prefer to read silently and all children should be encouraged to do so as much as possible.

(iii) Materials

The first priority is that reading should involve a genuine text, that is one which is written primarily to fulfil a particular communicative function, other than 'the introduction and practice of twenty new words'. Such texts alone can supply a full context in which the repertoire of skills and strategies can be used and honed to greater effectiveness.

It is necessary to offer a definition of communicative validity. A text is communicatively valid if three conditions are satisfied.

(a) The purpose of the text should be seen as reasonable by both writer and reader.
(b) Both reader and writer should wish to participate in the communication.
(c) The form of the text should not unnecessarily or unreasonably flout the principles of effective communication.

Communicative validity is not purely an intrinsic quality of text. Text which is valid for one person may not be for another (for example, one who 'doesn't like that kind of story'). On the other hand, text which appears to have little validity (for example, Graded Word Recognition Tests) may in fact be valid *if* the reader is prepared to enter into the game. Tests are a very unusual text form since their prime motivation is not to inform, but to assess the reader. Test construction is often influenced more by constraints of standardization or target of assessment than by the desire to communicate effectively.

Two principles of text construction, validity and simplicity have a particular relationship. All texts should be communicatively valid, and some will need to be simple. Simplicity measured on readability formulae is insufficient, as it makes no allowance for the textual, psychological and pragmatic factors. Text which is simple, in the narrowly defined terms of formulae, can be communicatively ineffective, inept or even bizarre.

One approach to literacy which is significantly different from the traditional reading scheme is the language experience technique. In terms of the interactive reading model, this approach is excellent, since the content is relevant and in addition is lexically and syntactically familiar (being produced by the child). The message and its lexical/syntactic realization are directly related, and alternative realizations of the same content will help the child to realize that language is a tool which is at his service. Written style can be compared with oral style and their similarities and differences highlighted. This bridge between personal experience and literary style made through meaning rather than structural practice is one which must be made in order to become an effective reader.

(iv) Diagnosis in Reading

There are two truisms concerning diagnosis in reading. The first is that any form of assessment reflects certain assumptions regarding how the reading process works and what is important to find out. The second is that any test involves an artificial situation and therefore differs from 'real' reading. It is necessary to be aware of the ways in which diagnostic materials and techniques differ from 'real' materials and 'real' reading, in order to understand the potential distortions and/or omissions which are introduced by test materials.

Without entering into fine detail, certain questions need to be asked of any test material:

(a) Does the test use a complete discourse?
(b) Would the material be significant, or communicatively valid or authentic if it were met outside the test situation?
(c) Does the test involve obviously artificial tasks, such as multiple choice completion?
(d) To what extent can the reader be flexible, and use a variety of processes in reading the test?
(e) To what extent does the reader need to form his own interpretation, as opposed to 'mind-reading' in an attempt to determine what it is that the tester wants?
(f) Does the test differentiate between WHAT a child can do, and HOW he/she does it?

It is clear that the more informal the test, and the more valid the material, the more informative will be the result. Informal assessment, using natural text, can be undertaken, and sensitive interpretation of the process of reader-text interaction will yield as much insight as any mechanical test. Such formal tests can then be restricted to their most useful role, that of screening or of assessing group levels of attainment.

Conclusions

The discussion of good text, teaching techniques, materials and diagnosis touch upon areas which are the concern of all teachers, particularly those who explicitly teach reading.

One group of children is of particular concern — those children who have difficulty in learning to read. Much of the early experience of these children, in areas of literacy, is controlled by the teacher or another adult, and they are subject to continuous intervention, all of which will reflect the knowledge and value of the teacher or of the school.

It follows that, to the extent that the teacher or school

- does not consider language in relation to its communicative function, and considers merely structure
- uses a narrowly based curriculum
- uses materials which are unhelpful, boring or unauthentic
- does not consider the *social* context of language and its effects
- is not aware of factors or even the presence of factors

then that teacher or school may cause a child to enter or remain within a reading deprivation cycle from which he cannot escape. The greatest single antidote to such a handicap is the teacher's vision of teaching reading as exploratory, an ever-changing adventure, rather than a recipe with few ingredients.

References

Austin, J. (1962) *How To Do Things With Words.* Oxford, Oxford University Press.

Bates, E. and MacWhinney, B. (1979) 'A functionalist approach to the acquisition of grammar', in Ochs, E. and Schieffelin, B. (Eds) *Developmental Pragmatics* London, Academic Press, pp. 167–211.

De Beaugrande, R. (1980) *Text, Discourse and Process*, London, Longman.

De Beaugrande, R. (1981) 'Design criteria for process models of reading', in *Reading Research Quarterly*, 16, 2, pp. 261–315.

Dahl, O. (1976) 'What is new information', in Enkvist, N. E. and Kohonen, V. (Eds) *Reports In Text Linguistics: Approaches to Word Order*, Abo: Text Linguistics Research Group, pp. 37–50.

Daneš, F. (1974) 'Functional sentence perspective and the organization of the text.' In Daneš, F. (Ed.) *Papers on FSP* Prague, Academia, pp. 106–28.

van Dijk, T. (1977) *Text And Context*, London, Longman.
Downing, J. and Leong, C.K. (1982) *Psychology of Reading*, New York, Macmillan.
Glushko, R.J. (1981) 'Principles for pronouncing print: The psychology of phonography', in Lesgold A.M. and Perfetti, C.A. (Eds) *Interactive Processes in Reading*, Hillsdale, N.J., Academic Press, pp. 61–84.
Graesser, A. (1981) *Prose Comprehension Beyond The Word* New York, Springer Verlag.
Green G.M. and Morgan J.L. (1981) 'Pragmatics, grammar and discourse', in Cole, P. (Ed.) *Radical Pragmatics*, London, Academic Press, pp. 167–81.
Grice, H.P. (1975) 'Logic and conversation'. in Cole P. and Morgan, J. (Eds) *Syntax and Semantics 3: Speech Acts*, New York, Academic Press, pp. 41–58.
Halliday, M.A.K. and Hasan, R. (1976) *Cohesion in English*, London, Longman.
Hoey, M. (1983) *On the Surface of Discourse*, London, Allen and Unwin.
Lewis, G.E. (1982) 'Text structure, text processing and testing reading', *Midland Association for Linguistic Studies Journal*, 7, pp. 43–69.
Lewis, G.E. (1983) 'Childrens perception of dynamics in narrative prose', *Midland Association For Linguistic Studies Journal*, 8 pp. 31–48.
Perera, K. (1982) 'The assessment of linguistic difficulty in reading material', and 'The language demands of school learning' in Carter, R. (Ed.) *Linguistics and the Teacher*. London, Routledge and Kegan Paul, pp. 101–13 and 114–36.
Reid, J.F. (1983) 'Into print: reading and language growth.' in Donaldson, M., Grieve, R. and Pratt, C. (Eds) *Early Childhood Development and Education*, Oxford, Blackwell, pp. 151–65.
Rumelhart, D.E. (1977) 'Towards an interactive model of reading.' in Dornic, S. (Ed.) *Attention And Performance VI*, Hillsdale, N.J., Erlbaum.
Schallert, D.L. (1980) 'The role of illustration in reading comprehension.' in Spiro, R.J., Bruce, B.C. and Brewer, W.F. (Eds) *Theoretical Issues in Reading Comprehension*, Hillsdale, N.J., Erlbaum, pp. 503–24.
Searle, J. (1969) *Speech Acts*, Cambridge, Cambridge University Press.
Urquhart, A. (1983) 'Sticky aspects of cohesion', *Midland Association For Linguistic Studies Journal*, 8, pp. 86–104.
Woods, W.A. (1980) 'Multiple theory formation in speech and reading.' in Spiro, R.J., Bruce, D.C. and Brewer, W.F. (Eds) *Theoretical Issues in Reading Comprehension*, Hillsdale, N.J., Erlbaum, pp. 59–86.

Part 5. Literacy Learning

Introduction

Each chapter in this final section fits within the framework of the volume and also introduces an important new dimension. The first of these chapters by Kemp in Australia, which was written for this publication, has as its theme the importance of the cohesiveness of any system of help for children with learning difficulties. Jansen from Denmark, in the final chapter considers the dangers in assuming that concepts are universal — or are even directly translatable in time or across languages.

The contribution of parents and the home to children's developing literacy is a theme which has been apparent in earlier chapters. Kemp, in the following chapter, discusses some of the more recent studies of parental involvement. He notes that it did not appear as had been anticipated that parental apathy was the stumbling block, instead it was the parents' awareness of their lack of skills rather than their lack of motivation, and on occasion teachers' unconvinced and defensive attitudes. Convinced of the importance of 'cohesiveness in a system of help' for children with reading difficulties and of the dangers that personnel in attempting to help may indeed pull in different directions, Kemp, Director of the Language Reading Centre in Canberra, developed a programme which enlisted the cooperation of parents as part of the 'system' to support the children's development towards literacy. The aim within this resource model which he describes was to minimize the withdrawal from normal classroom activities of children with reading difficulties and to maximize the help by all who can contribute, including the parents upon whom the work in the Centre was focused. The resource model presented by Kemp has the strength of utilizing additional, often untapped, resources. By explicit discussion of the aims of the instruction at the different stages it avoids the trap of misunderstandings leading efforts to help pulling the child in different directions, and not least it has potential for bringing into closer harmony teachers and parents of children with difficulties.

Jansen stresses the dangers in thinking that the concepts within which we consider a topic are either universal, or 'the most meaningful way to look at the world'. *Reading* was *not* the same at different historical times and it is not the same concept at different places in the world to-day. Furthermore, 'what is right at one level of teaching reading may be inefficient at another level of teaching reading and wrong at yet another'.

In order to succeed as a teacher of reading as of any other cognitive activity it is important that you are 'open to many possible solutions while the *work* is in progress' (also the 'play' in teaching reading). It is not either/or, as Jansen so persuasively argues, it is seriousness *and* fun; play *and* work, basics *and* creativity!

Parents as Teachers of Literacy

Max Kemp

Prologue

For four weeks Sara had attended our parents' training course with her husband. She and Philip were helping their 11 year old son Ben with his reading and writing. During these two-hour training sessions Sara had said nothing during discussions, but she had participated interestedly, leaving the talking to Philip.

It was clearly a struggle for Philip to stop himself from drifting out of the proceedings. He asked the occasional question, staying alert for the odd moment when he could say 'Yes, Ben's like that,' or 'We've done that too, but he lost interest in it.' Sara looked to Philip to speak for her but it was obvious from her keener attention that she was optimistic about Ben's chances and that the sessions were important to her.

On the fifth night we were talking about how to arrange the household chores and television times so that there would be quietness when the home teaching sessions were to begin. 'That's no good for Ben', Sara almost shouted. She looked around, startled at what she had said, and visibly retreated.

'Why not?' another parent asked. Sara's nervousness was obvious for a moment but she went on to explain that the only way Ben would test himself through reading aloud was above the rattle and crash of the washing up. As long as she would keep the noise going, Sara said, Ben was prepared to read to her and let her help him with the difficult parts.

After that night Sara was relaxed, confident and poised. She raised questions and gave answers and brought evidence of working purposefully with Ben at home. Philip too was less anxious. During the following months we watched Ben's transformation from an unhappy, semi-literate, misbehaving school avoider into a boy who couldn't find enough hours in the day to practise his story writing and reading.

Sara too had progressed since our first 'phone conversation, when I suggested to her that we would help her to teach Ben.

'Me?' she said. 'I'm just a mum. I couldn't do that.'

Introduction

Contexts of Remedial Teaching of Literacy

In a recent article on remedial teaching of literacy, Sophia Holmes (1982) provides a number of cameos of people whose attempts to give or receive information and help are affected by gaps and breakdowns in the fabric of assistance.

Holmes uses these sketches to show that the quality of a remedial teaching programme may hinge upon the particular amalgam of help that can come from several sources and is not merely the outcome of having a teacher available. She illustrates how a system of assistance may need to have cohesiveness from many fronts if remedial teaching — sometimes not available in a school at all — is to get the expected results. Holmes gives examples where the separate parts of a support system such as specialist teaching, expert counselling, cooperative parenting, and efficient administrative and procedural functions have had the potential for bringing about improvements, but have been ineffective. The failure has been due to procedures or personnel having pulled in different directions or not cooperated at all. Holmes has described how, in most instances of breakdown, someone has not understood what was really required to bring the best out of the system as a whole and to keep it in working order until the client's learning problem has been carefully analyzed and described, and finally solved.

Illustrations of systems' breakdowns should be familiar to teachers, who often find themselves at the tail-end of the consultative line, or to administrators who have to respond to generalized complaints when a system is not working. They include such examples as:

- the school counsellor who assesses and judges the child's needs but asks the teacher to perform impossible feats of one-to-one teaching;
- the school principal who has unbounded faith in the remedial teacher's capabilities and overloads her with clients;
- the parent who blames all teachers past and present for the child's learning difficulties;
- the remedial teacher with a mind closed to the possibility that a different procedure might help a particular child;
- an expert counselling and guidance process which draws many

conclusions about the client's learning strategies and behaviours but doesn't effectively consult with teachers about ways of dealing with them; or

- a school which rigorously identifies the children in need of help but nullifies its work by creating a caste system, with 'slow learners' at the bottom.

In each of these hypothetical and obvious cases there is a system in need of repair but in others the breakdown may be less overt and more difficult to describe. In any case, knowing or describing do not in themselves constitute the repair.

A Rationale for an Alternative System

A System View: What Is It?

A system approach to management is a familiar concept to educational administrators. In recent years a system view of helping relationships has been practised in psychotherapy and the treatment of personal tensions. The purpose of a system approach is to take the emphasis off the client's having sole responsibility for bringing about change and to place it also upon those who affect and are affected by the client's needs. Each person and process within the client's relationships is potentially part of the system which may have to provide support and help bring about stability through change.

In a school setting, a child's failure to learn what the school aims to teach is obviously unsettling because the school clearly and often scrupulously values what it is teaching. Failure to learn these valued things may have far-reaching consequences for the child, the family, peers and teachers. Sometimes the failure is almost expected, with all the attendant social as well as learning consequences; sometimes it is quite unexpected and unusual within the family context, and the source of lasting disappointment. Failure, however, inevitably embraces the concerns of those who are close to the child and it affects their further expectations at least within the school setting.

When people who are important to the child become aware of a school failure there is a heightened sensitivity to it. Judgments tend to become more frequent about the child's performances. Whereas the successful may go about their business enjoying their masteries, sometimes initiating others' judgments of them, failing children cannot avoid scrutiny. Even such help as is given tends to focus upon what cannot be done or understood and eventually the constant proximity of failure makes the child feel that he must be in some way responsible for it. Thus failure becomes embedded by increasing anxiety and frustration in being unable to manage what is apparently simple to others. The behaviours that express these tensions and disappointments tend also to push help further and further away as parents, teachers, friends and the school as an entity become critical, defensive, helpless, inactive and even distant in the face of the child's apparent lack of progress. Eventually all parties might retreat into a self-protective rationalization of the failure. In such circumstances we have a system in reverse, one in which all participants seem to be negating effort.

To have a system approach to giving a child assistance in literacy is to focus not only on the repair of failures but to bring all professional and parental judgments to bear on using what the child knows and can do. A system approach is, in Holmes' view, a method of keeping everyone informed about possibilities and action that is currently undertaken, and of informing them of their part in sustaining an agreed-upon programme of teaching and personal support.

Holmes briefly touches upon some of the ways in which parents participated in support and teaching programmes developed from her system view of remedial teaching. We will explore some of these and other possibilities. To that end the Canberra College of Advanced Education (CCAE) programme will be described, focusing upon an extension of the system to include the re-training of teachers, the training of school counsellors and parents, and the integration of these within a resource system for helping children with literacy learning difficulties. Emphasis will be given to the strengthening of the system at home, through parents' skilled participation in preventative and corrective work with their children.

Parents' Roles in the System, Past and Present

Education in a generic sense — and certainly particular components of it — has been the dominion of experts whose work has given them, by convention, some presumed rights of exclusive practice. However, it has not been easy for teachers to carve out the status of a profession because all people may (and seemingly do, on occasions) claim to have expert knowledge of what schools should do, might do and fail to do either in particular or general. This condition is arguably desirable, because the schools and their immediate societies need to coalesce to a considerable extent in the broad aims they pursue in their children's formal education. Whilst there are continual arguments about the changes that should take place in the balance between social and educational aims in (generally) industrialized countries, there is one school aim that the society never questions and indeed enshrines as a basic human and social right. That aim is to make everyone at least functionally literate.

The literacy aim is one which, although it continues to be hotly contested in terms of expected, minimal achievable standards, is rarely debated publicly with any substance. It is understood that there can be no such thing as a minimal acceptable standard, but perhaps it is a measure of a society's concern about literacy as a basic right that its newspapers nurse periodic controversies about claims of 'declining standards' of literacy, and that they muster arguments for and against schools' approaches to effective teaching.

Hence, committees of review, from Plowden to Bullock and Warnock in England, and the House of Representatives Committee in Australia (1976) have, during the last twenty years, gathered and expressed views about schools' expectations and management of the literacy curriculum. There has been a long-term educational consequence of these enquiries and their attendant controversies. The assumption that 'teachers know best' has become increasingly under challenge (Blackstone, 1979) and literacy must soon take its place with, for example, health as a topic for more public (as distinct from professional) investigations of when and how it may be acquired, what the literacy curriculum shall contain in its various levels and how its components might be taught, particularly in early schooling.

Readiness for Literacy

For decades, schools have been protected to some extent by a conventional wisdom about the timing and nature of the first teachings of literacy. Early developmental psychology emphasized the educational concept of 'readiness' for learnings of various kinds, and 'readiness to read' was chief amongst formal school learnings to be researched and described. Throughout the decades, pre-school and primary school teachers were instructed in the art of developing children's readiness to read and write, and a particular formality of approach was developed which tried to ensure that children would not read until they were deemed to be ready.

So formalized did teachers' training in this matter become that pre-school teachers were constrained not to over-step the bounds of professional ethics by teaching what was considered to be the infants' teacher's prerogative, that of the reading and writing curriculum. There is now developing an increasing sensitivity in some schools and in teacher education circles to the very individualistic nature of literacy learning, and to the dynamics of learning styles, the effects of family and social interactions, and the functions of oral language and natural exposure to print in predisposing children to readiness to read before they ever reach school (Clark, 1976).

Nevertheless, a residual conventional wisdom still holds at a public level. Some, perhaps many, parents and some teachers still believe that any advances into literacy that their children might make before they attend school could be disadvantageous. 'How will she fill in her time at school if she can already read?' is a worrying question indeed, not because it is going to get, very often, an equivocal answer but because it needs to be asked at all.

It is still something of a problem in some schools, even school systems, to be a 'young fluent reader' (Clark, 1976) arriving for the first school day.

Developmental Literacy

Parents who are worried because their children can already do what the school is supposed to teach them in reading and writing have an advantage not enjoyed by the greater number who must wait upon the school to run its customary course and teach literacy through its formal programme. Because the learning and teaching of literacy are age-related, and based upon the profession's collective knowledge about children's developmental characteristics, the arbitrary decisions about the timing and techniques of literacy teaching turn out to be favourable to most children's styles and rates of learning. There is a system, in other words, which suits the majority. But this controlling, locked-in condition is not like those of developmental learnings, such as talking (which on the face of it should be much more complex), social development and play. It allows for less self-monitoring, less evolution, less approximation to skill through experimentation and reflection, and less talking about what is being learned. The condition is an institutional one which, in traditional school settings, locks in teachers as well as learners.

If we were to consider that literacy learning could be more developmental in nature than it currently is, we would need to consider also how and whether some aspects of it might be unlocked and moved from school to pre-school and home. As well, we would need to consider whether all or only some homes could assume and manage the same sort of role in literacy as happens in their children's development of talking. If parents and others were to be trained to be part of the literacy system, who would do it and how? And how far might education authorities go (if at all) in devolving the schools' current responsibilities upon parents for their children's development into reading and writing? Lastly, how does the teacher, the person who must ensure the fluid working of the system, professionally guarantee that those who need special care in their literacy development will get it?

Evidence for Change

Bringing Home and School Together in Literacy Teaching

An effective literacy teaching support system must cater for three groups of children: the advanced; the amorphous 'average' group who, as much as the others, are individualistic in their rates and styles of learning; and the slow developers. It must fulfil these through three-roles — a preventative, a surveillance, and a corrective role, each of which is concerned with 'the system' as it must operate efficiently for all children.

The first, preventative role gives emphasis to schools helping parents to recognize and act upon those conditions which will enable reading and writing to evolve naturally and in harmony with their children's growing awareness of detail, and enjoyment of language and stories. This means that schools do not wait until the child begins school on the first day before they think about readiness to read and the programmes designed to elicit readiness. It means the schools' participation in community education, when parents are shown how to apply to literacy learning the same principles that they naturally and competently apply to their child's learning of oral language. It means pre-schools' and infant schools' accessibility to parents and to each other as resources and organizers of community participation. It also means planning and commitment from the profession, rather than the usually piece-meal attempts to explain the school's literacy curriculum on occasional parent-teacher nights.

The second, surveillance role gives emphasis to schools knowing every child and parent before and during the early years of schooling. It is the teaching profession's particular skill that it will know what to look for in the assessment of children's development in literacy, will know how to make judgments about children's competencies as distinct from their deficiencies, and will know how to use its knowledge to guide and support parents when this is needed.

The third, the corrective role, emphasizes the school's capacity to plan, execute and sustain action which will smooth the way for any child who has difficulties in learning to read and write. The corrective role will involve all participants and procedures in the system to change the conditions which are inhibiting a child's expected growth and development.

It would be wrong to persist with any implication that these prevention, surveillance and corrective roles are separate or mutually exclusive in nature. All actions to correct are preventative in intent; all preventative actions try to correct for possible imbalances and errors; and each type of action is an outcome of continuous professional surveillance. None of the three roles can function at an optimal level, however, without administrators, counsellors, parents and teachers being key members of the system as it applies to a particular child.

There is a slowly developing reservoir of reports and descriptions pertaining to the generally successful involvement of parents in literacy teaching. Most of them describe parents in the corrective role. However, the results of one study in which parents 'coached' their children by regularly listening to them reading (Hewison and Tizard, 1980; Tizard,

Schofield, and Hewison 1982) were so dramatic and unexpected that the experimenters subsequently developed a programme in which parents were switched into a more preventative role with equally dramatic success in application to curriculum development (Tizard, 1981). In the United Kingdom, in what have become known as the Dagenham Study and the Haringey Reading Project, and elsewhere the Belfield Reading Project (Jackson and Hannon, 1981), studies have shown that working class parents, the not-so-literate as well as the literate, and non-English speaking as well as native speakers, may make the need for corrective systems less abundant. In other places the research evidence is almost as compelling if not so large-scale. Glynn (1980) in the UK, and with collaborators in New Zealand (McNaughton, Glynn and Robinson, 1981); Sartain (1981), reporting on many projects in the USA and elsewhere which successfully used peers as well as parents; and Brown and Richardson (1978) in Australia, have all indicated that parent involvement in literacy education may be effectively extended beyond their customary menial activities in schools.

In each of the projects cited, as well as in many others not included here, the schools' researchers' initiatives can be seen as a response to the failure of a system to meet its obligations to a proportion of children, varying in different places from just a handful to, in others, a quarter or more of a school population deemed to be illiterate, semi-literate or markedly under-achieving in literacy development. In each case the initiatives were taken because parents were seen to be better placed than teachers in some respects for giving personal, one-to-one support for their children.

Generally, and with hindsight regrettably, teachers have not welcomed parent participation in classrooms at junior school level (and certainly not beyond) except in the more 'helper' and menial roles. Most parent participation is concerned with keeping extra curricular functions running smoothly (Cyster, Clift and Battle, 1980). When teachers have been asked to consider an extension of parents' roles into their classrooms they have been for the most part tentative, unconvinced of its value and perhaps defensive of their position of professional responsibility. Indeed many reactions of teachers are much stronger than that. Arguments have been put that training parents takes up more time than teachers can afford, that parents get in the way, are unskilled, may be critical of the school, or are too pushy or apathetic. Such views, given many times to the writer, express a common, if limited, perception of the functions of both teaching and parenting.

The most common argument given against the participation of parents in literacy teaching either at home or school, that of parent 'apathy', should be considered alone. It is applied often to parents in poorer socio-economic districts as well as to those of ethnic and colour differences, where the incidence of literacy problems is highest. The

NFER Report mentioned above (Cyster *et al.*, 1980) indicated that parents, far from being apathetic, were unable to contribute more than they were actually doing.

Pre-school teachers' comments too, should be contrasted with those of primary and secondary teachers: the former normally maintain close contact with parents in a flexible, interdependent ethos that focuses on individual children's experiences, learning and development (Blackstone, 1979) and whilst some parents of pre-school children may appear to be uninterested, this is rare. Other reasons, which may be attributed to professional inhibition, are more likely to explain the appearance of apathy. Glynn (1981), writing about the need for psychologists to make links between home and school for the benefit of better understanding children's circumstances had this to say:

> Home visits by the researchers established that parents were not apathetic. They were intensely concerned at their children's lack of progress, and wanted to help them. We learned in one study that the reported apathy of parents may sometimes be produced by negative encounters with the school system. We learned that, despite financial hardship and stress, what was lacking was not motivation to help their children, *but the specific skills necessary for success*. We found these parents also lacked the particular skills needed to approach teachers and school staff in order to get information about their children's progress and to obtain concrete help. (p. 5, my emphasis)

When the school is seen by parents to be actively interested in them and their children, and to be making an effort to involve them in the school's reading programme, parents 'almost without exception' (to use Tizard, Schofield and Hewison's empirically justified description) welcome the effort and are prepared to participate. Hewison's further commentary about the effectiveness of parents' participation (Hewison, 1982) also indicates that improvements in reading which take place because parents are involved, are likely to be more substantial and to last longer than improvements that occur because of teacher intervention at school.

While the evidence in favour of parent participation in the literacy curriculum mounts, teachers' flexibility on the issue remains problematical. On the one hand there are schools such as Campsbourne (Cadmean Trust, 1983) and Belfield (Jackson and Hannon, 1981) and districts such as Coventry (Widlake and McLeod, 1984) in England which have made demonstrable efforts to make the literacy curriculum a school-and-community project, while the majority continue to preserve a traditional structure which generates a nominal 10 per cent literacy problem rate. Perhaps teachers are concerned to preserve the traditional separateness for the reasons implied earlier: the profession will be weakened by an influx of amateurs; the system we currently have is manageable if not completely successful; the conventional wisdom has not been proved to be running counter to what we know about average learners; literacy is not a developmental learning in the strict sense; and the school knows best how to order its teaching.

One could tease out the truths and half-truths embedded in each of these assumptions, but this would not necessarily lead to the correction of faults in current modes of remediation. The effective prevention, surveillance and correction of what is arguably a professional weakness — that of allowing a continuing proportion of children to remain semi-literate or illiterate — can happen only if there is a marked change in the way we utilize all of the available resources and generate a system which is based upon all members of it being informed and mutually supporting.

Holmes' views about 'the system' which were described earlier, are in accord with the currently favoured 'resource model' (Bauer, 1975) of remedial teaching. The resource model is one which minimizes children's withdrawal for specialist teaching (which, we would recall, Hewison suggests is less immediately effective and less stable in the long term than parent coaching) and maximizes the preventative role of all who can contribute, be they teachers, other children or parents. The resource model proposes that the specialist teacher is a demonstrator and guide to those who are best able to give consistent, individual help to those children who need it in their everyday setting. Its effective development as an alternative system will require that teachers should think anew about their roles, and be prepared for retraining in the real use of community resources. The consequences of a resource model for teacher education programmes should also be obvious.

A Pilot Programme

Integrating the System

The following programme represents an attempt to bring teachers, counsellors, children, and parents together in a corrective function in literacy. It is an attempt to broaden and fully use a system specially designed to bring professionals and parents into closer harmony.

For a decade a programme of remedial teaching in literacy had been made available to children with special needs through the post-graduate course in special education at Canberra College of Advanced Education (CCAE). It was the kind of programme which is sometimes used in institutes of teacher education to give students a supervised, on-campus practicum which should benefit both teacher and learner. At CCAE, the programme was offered through the Language/Reading Centre, a group of rooms with spaces for assessment, teaching, guidance and the housing of materials, linked by one-way screens and incorporating video and audio recording facilities.

The programme had always attempted to use and develop any means of integrating school and CCAE services, and some degree of interdependence had evolved over the years between the Counselling and Guidance service of the Australian Capital Territory Schools Authority and the Language/Reading Centre. Children with special needs in literacy were identified and assessed by school counsellors and referred to the CCAE for assistance. This assistance was given after school hours by teachers enrolled in the Special Education course, and the children were retained on the programme, sometimes for several semesters, until they were seen to be at least functionally literate. In 1983 the programme underwent a dramatic change in orientation and purposes. After considerable consultation between the CCAE Language/Reading Centre, School of Education and Special Education course personnel, and senior members of the Australian Capital Territory Schools Authority (ACTSA) the Language/Reading Centre programme was redesigned to take more effective account of the resource teaching model of special assistance and to bring about a more fully integrated 'system view' of remedial teaching of literacy. In short, ACTSA and the CCAE School of Education combined to develop a resource teaching course. The course structure was based upon agreed principles of a system approach to helping children with special needs. The Language/Reading Centre's role was to organize and sustain a practicum which would be consistent with these principles.

In doing this, it would try to integrate counselling and guidance personnel, parents of referred children, the children's teachers at school, and the children's CCAE postgraduate teacher/students. Emphasis would be given particularly to the guidance and training of parents, with the graduate teachers taking less of a key part in teaching an assigned child and more of key part in training the child's (or another) parent to do the teaching.

To assist the CCAE Language/Reading Centre meet its broadening aims, ACTSA appointed a teacher to the Centre. With full-time and part-time personnel available, the Centre's additional aims included two focal ones:

(i) to provide parents with a regular, structured programme of either individual or group sessions which would enable them to build their own teaching skills in aspects of literacy, and thereby support their children's literacy development at home;

(ii) to give graduate teachers parent-training experiences which would better fit them to undertake such programmes with parents in their own schools.

Three programmes were designed or reshaped from existing ones to help meet these aims from the start of 1983. They were:

(i) A day-time consultation between Centre staff and individual parents. These sessions included both parents if possible. They were conducted for approximately an hour each week, commencing with the child attending but generally tapering off the child's attendance as the parents' confidence and skill developed. Periodic 'recall' of the child was arranged to monitor progress, and the ACTSA teacher visited schools. Parents' skills were reviewed through micro-teaching sessions, using videotapes of sessions filmed through a one-way screen. Each session included a planning and review time for assisting the parents in programming their home sessions, which were scheduled to last for fifteen minutes only each week night.

(ii) An evening group training programme with parents who were unable to participate during the day. This programme included nine two-hour workshop sessions, using teaching materials and videotapes of techniques such as listening to reading, using correction strategies during reading aloud, assisting in process writing, helping with spelling, group interactions for mutual support, and parent-teacher communication strategies. Counsellors within the CCAE and school systems were available for home visits to parents who requested them.

(iii) A late afternoon programme of two hours each week for the children of parents who had completed a series of training sessions, but were still dependent upon professional assistance or felt that their child responded better to them at CCAE than at home.

The parents were referred to the Centre with their children by ACTSA school counsellors, who discussed with the parents the implications of their participation in a sustained training programme. These discussions had taken place generally at the child's school, with teachers and school principals being drawn into the referencing procedures. It is a measure of parents' interest that their reaction was almost invariably positive, indeed enthusiastic, and that many of them made complex adjustments to their routines and working hours to fit in with the programmes' schedules. The parent population included those with very high professional and tertiary qualifications and others who were early school leavers, many of whom had a first language other than English.

Central to the programme was the participation of graduate teachers and a number of pre-service students who had a particular interest in working with children with special needs. Their supervised work with parents as well as children was designed to help them to assess and constructively use parents as a key resource in the development of a system view of resource teaching with literacy having the particular priority.

Parents, Teachers and Children: Some Outcomes of a System Approach

Two years after the implementation of the system approach to remedial help through the CCAE Language/Reading Centre, some tentative judgments can be made. The three interlocking programmes have attempted to approach remedial assistance in literacy on several fronts, each one of them being in sight of and informing the other. In taking a resource-teaching, system view of helping children with reading and writing difficulties, the major thrust of the programmes has been to distribute specialist professional knowledge more evenly amongst those who are affected by a child's inability so far to profit from what the school is trying to do. In addition the professionals have gathered information and support from those who are elsewhere affected by the child's slow development into literacy, particularly the child's parents. Teachers, parents, children, school counsellors, school principals and a teacher education programme have as a consequence of the system, gained different facets of experience of bringing support to children with special needs in literacy. The programme has catered throughout the two years for 120 families and the demand for assistance shows no sign of abating.

The programme lends itself to research in a number of avenues and some studies have been begun. These include the measurement of parental responses to the programme, using pre- and post-programme attitudinal scales; and children's pre- and post-programme social and home behaviours as assessed on an observational scale. Literacy growth of the children is assessed less by standardized achievement tests than by cumulative records of achievement in all aspects of literacy. (A major reason for not using standardized tests is the fragile nature of children's responses until it is obvious by all realistic measures that a child can read and write). The programmes were monitored in 1983 by an independent observer (Seaton, 1984) the focus being placed upon an ethnographic study of parents' responses to the programmes' aims, content and presentation.

In the long term it will become apparent whether the development of a resource-teaching and system approach, as exemplified in the CCAE/ACTSA mode, justifies the faith that has been placed in parents to help in the corrective role of literacy teaching in schools.

The evidence is accumulating that parents are very effective in the preventative role when the school makes positive efforts to work with them. It is the schools' responsibility to sustain the surveillance role and to ensure that those who are at risk are given the most suitable teaching that the system can devise. Meanwhile, many parents who may see themselves as presently outside the school system could prove to be a sound investment in schools' attempts to broaden the structure of corrective teaching in literacy. Hewison and Tizard's citation of the forward-thinking but tentative Plowden Report is apposite, when they say that what matters ultimately is '... whether there is a genuine mutual respect, whether parents understand what the schools are doing for their individual children and teachers realize how dependent they are on parental support.' (Plowden Report, 1967)

References

BAUER, H. (1975) 'The resource teacher — a teacher consultant', Academic Therapy, 10, 3, Spring.

BLACKSTONE, T. (1979) 'Parental involvement in education', *Education Policy Bulletin*, University of Manchester, 7, 1, Spring, pp. 81–98.

BROWN, J. and RICHARDSON, J. (1978) 'Educational counselling of parents of poor readers', *Australian Journal of Reading*, 1, 2, pp. 67–74.

CADMEAN TRUST (1983) 'Crossfire — partnership for reading' — 16 mm. film produced for and distributed by *Cadmean Trust*, London.

CENTRAL ADVISORY COUNCIL FOR EDUCATION, (1967) *Children and Their Primary Schools* (Plowden Report), London, HMSO.

CLARK, M.M. (1976) *Young Fluent Readers*, London, Heinemann Educational Books.

CLAY, M.M. (1979) *Reading: The Patterning of Complex Behaviour*, (2nd edn), Heinemann Educational, Auckland.

CYSTER, R., CLIFT, P.S. and BATTLE, S. (1980) *Parental Involvement in Primary Schools*, Windsor, NFER.

GLYNN, T. (1980) 'Parent-child interaction in remedial reading at home' in CLARK, M.M. and GLYNN, T. (Eds), *Reading and Writing For the Child with Difficulties*, Educational Review, Occasional Paper No. 8, University of Birmingham.

GLYNN, T. (1981) 'New directions in the work of educational psychologist' closer involvement with parents', *Exceptional Child*, 28, 1, March, pp. 3–18.

HEWISON, J. (1982) 'Parental involvement in the teaching of reading', *Remedial Education*, 17, 4, pp. 156–62.

HEWISON, J. and TIZARD, J. 'Parental involvement in reading attainment', *British Journal of Educational Psychology*, 50, pp. 209–15.

HOLMES, S. (1982) 'Failure to learn: A system view', *Australian Journal of Family Therapy*, 4, 1, pp. 27–35.

HOUSE OF REPRESENTATIVES COMMITTEE. (1976) *Report of Inquiry into Learning Disabilities (Cadman Report)*, AGPS, Canberra.

JACKSON, A. and HANNON, P. (1981) *The Belfield Reading Project*, Rochdale, Belfield Community Centre.

MCNAUGHTON, S., GLYNN, T. and ROBINSON, V.M. (1981) *Parents as Remedial Reading Tutors*, Wellington, New Zealand Council for Educational Research.

SARTAIN, H.W. (1981) *Mobilizing Family Forces for World Wide Reading Success*, Research Summary: Family Contributions to Reading Attainment, Newark, Del, International Reading Association.

SEATON, B.C. (1984) 'An evaluation of the parent training evening seminar group program in the language/reading centre at the Canberra College of Advanced Education', MEd Field Study, CCAE.

TIZARD, B., MORTIMORE, J. and BURCHALL, B. (1980) *Involving Parents in Infant and Nursery Schools: A Source Book for Teachers*, Grant McIntyre.

TIZARD, J., SCHOFIELD, W.N. and HEWISON, J. (1982) 'Collaboration between teachers and parents in assisting children's reading', *British Journal of Educational Psychology*, 52, 1, pp. 1–15.

WIDLAKE, P. and MCLEOD, F. (1984) *Raising Standards: Parent Involvement Programmes and the Language Performance of Children*. Community Education Development Centre, Coventry, L.E.A.

*Language and Concepts: Play or Work? — Seriousness or Fun? — Basics or Creativity?**

Mogens Jansen

Either-or?

It is a fundamental misunderstanding that seriousness and fun are contrary terms. Just as wrong as the watertight distinction between work and play, working hours and leisure time — they are labels. It was not like that at all in the stone age, I guess, and not at all in the Garden of Eden? But it is necessary to be reminded that even such a well-defined distinction is not in the things themselves. It is in the categories we make of them. Most of the readers of this article would link creativity and play — I guess. 'That must be the right thing!' But that is wrong. We can easily find other groups of teachers who would underline basic skills and work. And it is correct that this is also wrong.

The question has been asked wrongly, and to a wrongly asked question one may at the most expect an unreasonable answer. The questions are asked, as if you had to answer by an either/or:

'Rich or poor?'

'Thick or thin?' — 'Well, it depends on with whom you are comparing him. I think that he is maybe a little thinner than thicker.'

'Would you like pears or apples for dessert?' — and you prefer strawberries!

Either/or questions are not at all always meaningful. Personally, I think that they are seldom meaningful!

When once in a while I visit the United States and hear people discussing the two parties, Democrats and Republicans, I cannot choose — considering that we have about ten political parties in the Danish

* Originally published in a longer version in *International Research in Reading*, 1, 1, 1984.

Parliament and some outside. I think again: either/or questions are meaningless.

Why Either/Or?

But why these either/or questions? Is it *a linguistic tradition* based on a thinking which is deep-rooted in 'either/or'? Or is it *the thinking which rests on the language?* — What was first: the hen or the egg? As far as I know, they were there at the same time; and at least without the one, there is not the other.

Maybe it is the language which creates our problems? — And what I want to stress is some considerations about the language as boxes into which we put our thinking. These boxes may be all right. Maybe they are meaningful — Sometimes. But I am sure that very often they cause much confusion. We *think* our language is the language which has to be used — and yet there are many other possibilities. We *think* our own environments are the surroundings which have to constitute the framework of our concepts — but maybe there are more suitable possibilities? We *think* our concepts are universal — or at least the most meaningful way to look at the world — and yet they are but the poor results of our narrow backgrounds.

I would like to give an example: many contemporary American educators regard the terms skill, skills, skill training with a deep mistrust — and, according to what I have seen in American schools, rightly so. However, when these words are translated into Danish, they represent something valuable. The explanation is that even if we translate word for word, an American skill, it is — I am tempted to say — a very small isolated fraction of a Danish skill. We have different systems of measurement and different currencies. We also have rather greater differences, when it comes to, for example, skills. Educationally, a Danish skill is a large and comprehensive unit which can be trained rationally and advantageously and into which many subskills enter. These subskills cannot be trained separately. But it is just these subskills that are trained in the American school. The concept of subskills in fact does not exist in Danish at all!

Are Our Languages the Problem?

Our languages sometimes make us form wrong images of reality; but equally they may help us see a deeper connection. It is already a source of error that we think: One word = one concept. One concept = one word. This is bound to lead us astray.

It is a valuable advantage to move among more than one language;

concepts are not tyrannized quite so much by words; they are, to some degree, loosened from them, because the words in the different languages do not mean quite the same things. For example, look at the scheme in Figure 1. which deals with so concrete and substantial a matter as wood — something tangible. And by the way we have still more words in English. What about woods?

Figure 1.

<table>
<tr><th>English</th><th>Danish</th><th>Swedish</th><th>French</th></tr>
<tr><td>tree</td><td rowspan="2">træ</td><td>träd</td><td>arbre</td></tr>
<tr><td>wood</td><td rowspan="2">trä
skog</td><td>bois</td></tr>
<tr><td>forest</td><td>skov</td><td>forêt</td></tr>
</table>

Everyone knows what wood means, and everyone knows what tree means — not to mention forest! These three words make sense. It is either one or the other, or, in this case, perhaps the third.

However, in my language we have only two words to cover the same. And when I speak German or French, I have three words — but they are not similar to the three in English.

The groupings are different. Maybe in this connection the basic problem is that we have had too little forest in Denmark? Maybe! But . . . at the time when the words came into the Danish language — when they were created in the language and in our thinking — we did have a great deal of forest! Denmark was covered with forest? Or was it wood? Or woods? This actually creates problems for translation and in an international conversation.

When this topic is discussed in Danish, it is either 'træ' (= wood) or 'skov' (= forest), but the words mean something different in Swedish which is linguistically close to Danish, and Sweden is geographically close to Denmark. At the time when the words were created they were neighbouring countries rather like the northern states of the United States are to the southern provinces of Canada. And in the Danish 'skov' (forest) if our 'skov' were English there are parts of both wood and forest.

As another example, we could choose something which is even better known.

What about these words? — I give them in Danish and English; they cover the same concepts — grøn, blå, grå, brun (= green, blue, grey, brown). (See Figure 2)

If you look at the same words in Cymric, the Welsh language, you will wonder how much blue they had in the old Celtic Wales! And apparently these people could not distinguish between grey and brown!

The Danish king, Harold Bluetooth, who reigned from AD 950–985

Figure 2.

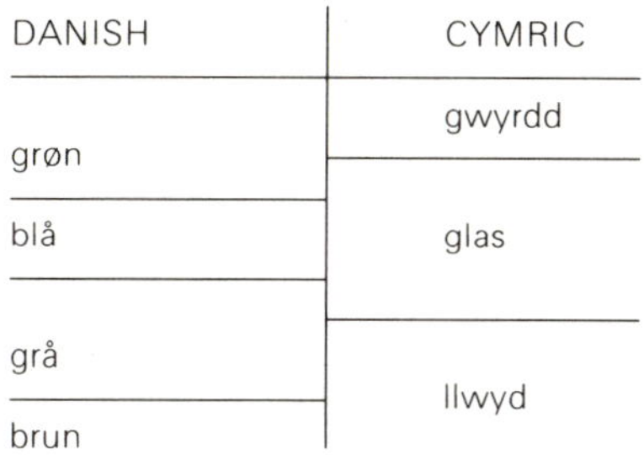

Source: DALBY, M.A., ELBRO, C., JANSEN, M., KROGH, T. and CHRISTENSEN, W.P. (1983) *Bogen om Læsning I — Forudsoatninger Ag Status*, Købenaun, Munksgaard. og Danmarks Pædagogiske Institut.

had probably no blue teeth. And the people from North Africa with whom the Vikings fought were hardly painted blue, even if the Vikings called them Bluebacks. Perhaps the problem was that the Vikings could not tell blue from black. Or maybe they divided the colour range differently. And did they have a different standard of value from the Englishmen and the Bluebacks (the Moors) with whom they did not always keep on good terms?

It is said that the Eskimos have twenty-six words for love. But they do have many, many words for snow: wet, dry, falling, packing, frozen, and so on. If one has been to Greenland, one knows that this is so. It is of no use saying: either it snows, or it doesn't snow, for it snows in so many different ways.

It is like being in the Faroe Islands and asking a question about rain or dry weather knowing that there are a minimum of ten, maybe twenty words, for rain and at least as many for all the different degrees of dry weather.

It may well be language that creates our problems. So perhaps it is language that can solve item.

Are the Concepts the Problem?

Behind words are concepts. Perhaps in this respect languages differ a little. Piet Hein says that in Danish it is almost impossible to say something serious without a different perspective being seen dimly behind it. And, fortunately, it is almost impossible to say something jocular in Danish without a glimpse of a serious background. You get some idea of this characteristic of the Danish language by reading Hans Andersen's fairy-tales. Even in translation you will find it present.

This fact points out to Danes that their language (and I guess that it is true of any language) is not suitable for everything. You have to be born in England in order to understand Alice in Wonderland. Even this is not enough, I think you need to be English with a very particular British tradition behind you. For me *Winnie the Pooh* is more universal. And yet I have tried in vain to explain to people outside North Western Europe why I like *Winnie the Pooh!* Is it the language or the concepts surrounding Pooh that get in the way?

Let us have a look at the concepts of 'seriousness' and 'fun'. These words or concepts are natural contrasts. But not in Danish. 'Seriousness' in Danish is a closed concept it conveys the idea of narrowness, of a subject exhausted, allowing for no other or wider perspectives.

And 'fun'? Fun is a waste of time but it is also a concept which keeps the mind open to alternative ideas; a gateway to other worlds. It is often said that languages create more problems that they solve. Perhaps it is true. It is also the case that languages provide us with possibilities of a richer life, more so if we thought less of either/or and more of both/and. In the long run I think it is the only way to survive — the world is growing smaller, and the boundaries are becoming more and more rigid. We don't understand each other.

Languages Contain Many Ideas — Children Grow and Learn — Reading Does Not Remain the Same As It Once Was.

Perhaps the greatest problem we create in reading is that we do not recognize that languages develop. That the child develops, grows, emerges, become more experienced, we know. By the same token we ought to teach reading on the basis of a knowledge that reading also is developing. 'Reading' was not the same concept at different times in history, and it is not the same concept at different places in the world today. What is right at one level of teaching reading may be insufficient at another level of teaching reading and wrong at yet another. Furthermore, the question of teaching reading is not a question of teaching *either* this way *or* that way, but in most cases of teaching *both* this way *and* that way. At least when you see it in relation to an individual's lifetime's experience. In consequence we must listen when we teach. Perhaps we must listen more than we teach. At any rate we must both listen and teach. We must try to hearken to the individual's development, note the different experiences of the individual, and try to be aware of the possibilities open to the individual. Reading education is not a matter of following rules. It is more a voyage of discovery for both teacher and taught.

The Essential Things are the Differences — 'both/and'

Not so long ago, teachers in my country were called 'hearers'. They heard the pupils recite what they had learned by heart, and this was the only correct method. 'This is not a training to become human beings, but to become ants in a community of ants', says Piet Hein (1966).

Our developing is due to our openness, our ability to learn new things and to expand our world. Put reading into this sentence, and you will surely see what I mean: the development of reading is due to openness, the ability to learn new ways of reading and to expand the world of reading.

In some countries there is a tradition that in teaching reading many teachers — particularly in special and remedial education — teach according to a 'bottom-up' model (see Figure 3); a model for teaching reading which has its uses in difficult schools and with beginning or less competent teachers.

Figure 3.

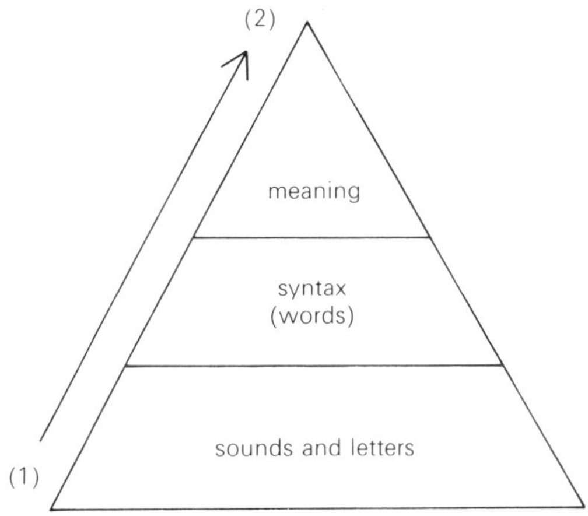

In practice meaning, syntax, sounds/letters are mingled and one cannot take anything from one of the three sectors without also getting something from the other two (see Figure 4). If one teaches according to the 'Bottom-up' model of teaching reading only, learning is built on meaningless material which will hardly prove functional in the long run. It will and must break down. For a method of teaching reading to function, it must be characterized by 'both/and'. The teaching must be both 'Top-down' and 'Bottom-up'. There needs to be both methods used in work with pupils.

A developmental theory of teaching reading where any of the three fields may be used as a starting point is needed. One which accepts that the three fields are connected, bound up with each other. In principle this model grows, widens in scope, opens possibilities of new strategies in teaching reading (see Figure 5).

Figure 4.

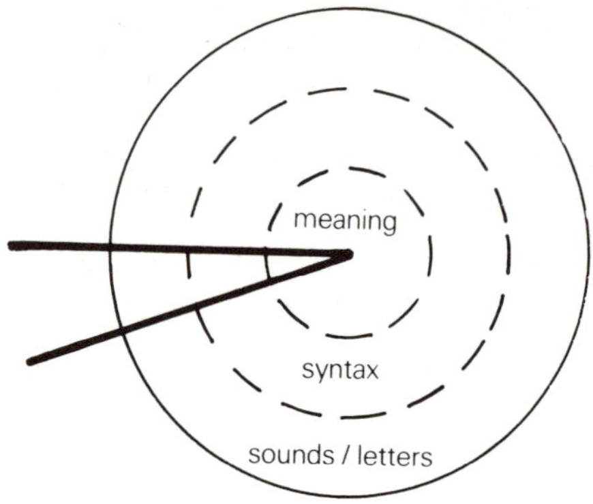

Figure 5.

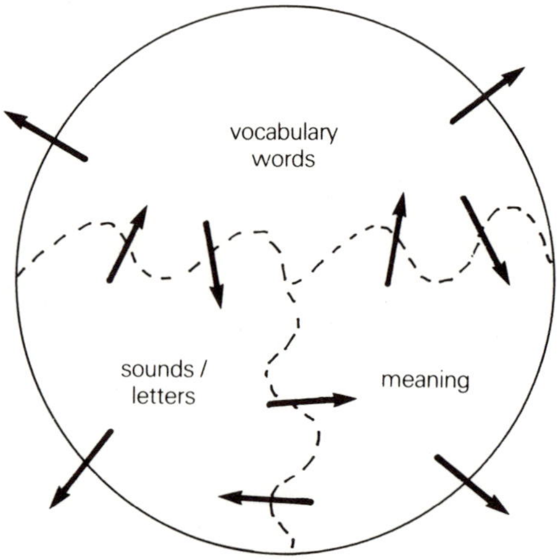

This approach, I would describe, as 'pragmatic'. It allows teaching to begin where the child is and this changes as the child's reading education progresses. It is essentially the teaching of reading without a planned method.

Paradoxically, if you think of '*either* this way *or* that way', you will never reach your goal. You must be open to many possible solutions, while the work is in progress. This is not less true in the teaching of reading than it is of education as a whole.

References

BLOCH, A. (1979, 1980 and 1982) *Murphy's Law,* I–III, Los Angeles, Price/

Stern/Sloan Publishers Inc.

DALBY, M.A., ELBRO, C., JANSEN, M., KROGH, T. and CHRISTENSEN, W.P. (1983) *Bogen om læsning I — forudsætninger og status*, København, Munksgaard og Danmarks pædagogiske Institut.

HEIN, P. (1966 and 1970) *Grooks*, København, Borgens Forlag, Pocketbooks 85 og 103.

HEIN, P. (1980) Leg er alvor. I, Olaf Thygesen Damm (red.), *Godt begyndt*, Billund, Lego System A/S, pp. 8–17.

JANSEN, M. (1982) 'All that is not said — in the reading research which we translate', *Journal of Research in Reading*, 5, 1, pp. 4–5.

JANSEN, M., JACOBSEN, B. and JENSEN, P.E. (1978) *The Teaching of Reading Without Really Any Method*, An analysis of reading instruction in Denmark, København, Munksgaard New Jersey, Humanities Press, Inc.

Contributors

Jennifer E. Barr is an Educational Psychologist in the Fife Region, Scotland.

Marion Blank is a Clinical Professor in the Albert Einstein College of Medicine, New York.

Margaret M. Clark is Professor of Education in the Department of Educational Psychology, University of Birmingham and a Past President of the United Kingdom Reading Association.

Margaret Donaldson is Professor of Developmental Psychology in the Department of Psychology, University of Edinburgh.

John Downing is Professor of Psychological Foundations of Education, University of Victoria, Canada, and a Past President of the United Kingdom Reading Association.

Emelia Ferreiro is Professor in the Department of Educational Research Centre for Advanced Studies, National Polytechnic Institute, Mexico.

Uta Frith is a member of the Senior Scientific Staff in the Medical Research Council Cognitive Development Unit, London.

Mogens Jansen is Research Director of the Danish Institute for Educational Research, Copenhagen, and President of the Danish National Association of Reading Teachers.

Max Kemp is Director of the Language/Reading Centre in the School of Education, Canberra College of Advanced Education, and is a Past President of the Australian Reading Association.

Geoffrey E. Lewis is Senior Lecturer in Educational Studies at Trent Polytechnic, Nottingham.

John A. McInnes was formerly Professor in the Ontario Institute for Studies in Education, Toronto.

John E. Merritt is Professor of Teacher Education, School of Education, in the Open University, Milton Keynes, and a Past President of the United Kingdom Reading Association.

John Pearce is Senior Area Inspector (Huntington) and Inspector of English, Cambridgeshire Local Education Authority.

Jessie Reid was formerly Senior Lecturer in the Department of Educational Sciences, University of Edinburgh.

Wendy Sutton is Headteacher of Perry Beeches Nursery School, Birmingham.

Margaret van Lierop is a member of the Multicultural Education Service, Wolverhampton.

Author Index

Subject Index